CALIFORNIA

Text by ROSANNA CIRIGLIANO

Photographs by ANDREA PISTOLESI

EB
BONECHI
SNCO

Distribution by

smith NOVELTY COMPANY
460 Ninth Street
San Francisco, CA 94103
U.S.A.
Phone: 415 - 861-4900

ISBN 0-938765-30-2

Printed in Italy by
Centro Stampa Editoriale Bonechi.

Text by Rosanna Cirigliano.

Photographs from the Archives of Casa Editrice Bonechi taken
by Andrea Pistolesi, *with the exception of the following*
photographs:

James Blank
pages: 24,37, 40, 62-63, 120 above, 137, 138 below, 141, 142, 143,
144.

Richard A. Bucich
page 84 below.

Stefano Cellai
page 131 below.

Ken Glaser Jr.
pages: 22, 23, 27, 53 above right and left, 78, 79 below,
145 above.

Peter Lik
page: 3.

Andrew McKinney
pages: 25, 26, 79 above.

A. Scott
page: 145 below.

© The Walt Disney Company
page: 135 - with permission of the Walt Disney Company.

The Publisher thanks the Universal Studios *and* The Walt Disney
Company *for their kind cooperation.*

Page 83: The "Lone Cypress Tree" photograph is reproduced by
permission of the Pebble Beach Company, all rights reserved.

* * *

Traveling Back in Time

Californians have always been a people on the move, starting with Hernán Cortés, the Spanish conqueror of Mexico. In 1535 Cortés sailed north in search of an island, according to the book Las Sergas de Espalandián by Garcia Ordóñez de Montalvo, "very close to the side of the Terrestrial Paradise." Instead, he became the first European, albeit in an unofficial capacity, to glimpse what he decided was the upper part of a "peninsula," an extension of today's "Baja California." In the 1500s, however, "Baja (lower) California" referred to Mexico, while "Alta California" was the territory that Cortés had sighted.

Most history books focus on the 1542 voyage of Portuguese seaman Juan Rodríguez Cabrillo, who sailed under the Spanish flag. The two ships he commanded dropped anchor near present-day San Diego, Santa Monica and San Pedro and other places along the California coast. Cabrillo's mission was twofold. He was looking for El Dorado, Spanish for "the gilded one," a place of legendary riches thought to exist somewhere in the New World. The odds were that El Dorado was somewhere in California, corresponding to de Montalvo's description that "...on the whole island, there was no metal but gold." Cabrillo was probably also on the lookout for the Northwest Passage, a shortcut to the wealth (and markets) of the Orient.

Sebastian Vizcaíno, another Portuguese skipper hired by the Spanish crown, stopped off in California on his way to Manila in 1602. He discovered Monterey Bay, and sung the praises of this natural harbor to such an extent that it later became a destination of the first Spanish overland party. In the

California's first Catholic church and mission, the **Mission San Diego de Alcala**, was consecrated on July 16, 1769.

meantime, however, English adventurer Sir Francis Drake with his Golden Hind arrived in 1579. He came ashore, it is believed, in Point Reyes (although Santa Barbara is another possibility), where, crowned by enthusiastic Indians, he claimed "Nova Albion" for Queen Elizabeth and "Herr Succesors Forever."

In 1763, the French and Indian War (as it was known in America) or the Seven Year's War (as it was known in Europe) established England's domination across the northern part of the New World. A worried, strongly Catholic Spain thus decided to send a military and religious expedition to finally settle "Alta California" during the second half of the same decade. Thus, the unlikely combination of spiritual and military might, represented by Franciscan friar Fra Junípero Serra and Gaspar de Portola, respectively, was to create Mission San Diego de Alcala, the first European outpost in Alta California (1769). Portola tried in vain to find Monterey Bay; instead his small band of troops discovered San Francisco Bay. California was taken from its Native American inhabitants practically without a shot having been fired. Serra, the "Apostle of California," succeeded in his intent of setting up missions along "El Camion Real" (the Royal Road) from San Diego up to Sonoma, but many of the submissive Indians who were baptized died of unknown diseases introduced by the white man. During the same period, the Russians were exploiting the fur trade in Alaska, and, lured by the abundance of California sea otters, founded a military outpost at Fort Ross, just north of present-day Jenner.

The flag of the newly-formed Republic of Mexico flew over Monterey, the capital of Alta California in 1822, and American politicians began to think that owning the territory could be highly advantageous. The Mexicans secularized the missions in 1833, and doled out millions of acres of mission-owned land to Spanish-American settlers known as Californios. The rancheros era in California was vividly portrayed by Henry Dana in his book Two Years Before the Mast. It was an era in which Yankee merchant seaman braved the long voyage from the East around the Straits of Magellan, and traded items necessary to every day life in exchange for a precious cargo of cattle hides. After a period of rising tension and border skirmishes, the U.S. declared war against Mexico on May 13, 1846. This prompted explorer John C. Fremont and a band of U.S. patriots in Sonoma to hoist the "Bear Flag" — a banner of a bear facing a red star — and proclaim the independent "Bear Flag Republic." The newly-founded nation lasted only until July 7, when U.S. naval officer John Drake Sloat sent an envoy ashore to demand that the military commandant of Monterey surrender. The Mexican army officer handed the matter in an extremely diplomatic fashion: he sent word that all his soldiers would simply withdraw from Monterey. Sloat raised an American flag over the Customs House and declared "henceforth California will be a portion of the United States."

The state was admitted to the Union in 1850; two years earlier John Marshall had found a gold nugget on property near Sacramento belonging to John Sutter, thus triggering a world-wide "Gold Rush." The population of San Francisco exploded from a few hundred to 25,000 in the space of three years, and spawned the fast-living, fast-dying "Barbary Coast." A "Silver Rush," smaller in scale, would place in the Sierra Nevada foothills at the end of the same decade.

The Sonoma Valley, site of the 1846 Bear Flag Revolt is now the site of premier vineyards which can be admired by taking a hot-air balloon excursion.

California's focus turned to agriculture, especially in the Central or San Joaquin Valley, wine making in the Napa and Somona valleys, as well as logging in the far North during the second half of the 19th century, and the local economy was boosted by ever-increasingly important railroad links. Chinese-Americans, Italians, and Portuguese joined California residents in setting up a thriving fishing industry. Then on April 18, 1906, early in the morning, San Francisco experienced a massive earthquake which killed 500 people and destroyed, together with the fire that followed it, much of the city. Slowly the town rebuilt and became bigger than before. At the same time, southern California became renowned as a vacation resort and the fledging capital of the movie industry, and oil was soon discovered offshore there. The 1920s and 1930s saw many a Californian still employed in reaping the bounties of agriculture, a pattern that was to change slightly during World War II, when the defense industry boomed. The 1970s and '80s brought the development of firms specializing in electronics and technology, exemplified by the Silicon Valley, and in service-related industries, while California as a vacation spot has never waned in popularity.

Geographic Shiftings

Californians live right on the edge, in a moral and often physical sense. Millions of years ago the state was completely underwater, and, due to the expulsion of molten rock from the earth's core,

To the north, the volcanic mountains of the Cascade Range are thought to be extinct, although the probability cannot be classified a certainty. The geographic shiftings in California which created the mountain ranges and the often rugged coastline and carved out the beautiful valleys continue still today.

mountain ranges were uplifted and a tectonic plate was formed that pushed against the far edge of the continent. Between the two is a network of cracks and fissures, the most prominent being the San Andreas fault, stretching 270 miles. The Bay Area sits squarely on the San Andreas fault, as testified by the occurrence of major earthquakes in 1906 and 1989.

Above, centuries ago, the earth's Ice Age produced the **Liberty Cap,** a major attraction in the **Yosemite Valley** in the Sierra Nevada mountains east of San Francisco. The seven-mile-long valley, full of natural granite monoliths and waterfalls, was not discovered by American settlers of European descent until 1851. Another natural wonder, the Sierra Nevada sequoia tree (sequoia gigantea) grows in the park's Mariposa Grove.

Impressions of the Golden State in Motion

Californians continue to be a people on the move into the second millennium. An interesting experiment would be to pick 15 Californians at random and invite them home for coffee, and analyze their ethnic, socio-economic backgrounds. A high probability exists that only three had been actually born in the state, a person with European roots, a Chinese-American and a Native American; some of the others, of European or African descent, will have migrated to California from the East Coast or the Midwest; several will definitely be of Asian origin, natives of Vietnam, Laos, Cambodia or the Philippines; and at least two will be Mexicans, one a legal resident and another in hiding from Proposition 187. A volatile mixture that doesn't always mix, proved by the fact that many of these groups live in self-contained enclaves. California's population today also reflects an ethnic separateness and toleration which is unique. People from all over the Pacific, from the Caribbean, South America and the rest of the Western Hemisphere all live next to each other, retaining their ethnic identity, but each also being a Californian. Many of the present Chinese-Americans are fourth or fifth generation Californians; their forefathers built California's railroads during the second half of the 19th century. They are traditionally high academic and career achievers. At the other end of the spectrum, a high percentage of Native Americans, sadly, lead marginal lives in reservations. The Asian-American in general is in the process of assimilation as regards traditional American culture and mores; the African-American and Mexican-American is less likely to be so. All have contributed to swell the population of California to 30,000,000 people in the 1990s, a figure that has nearly doubled in 30 years, when one realizes that the official head count in 1966 was 18,084,000. What attracts massive numbers of people in transit to California? Many came actively seeking the embodiment of El Dorado, the "Golden State," if not an earthly paradise, a place where they can fulfill their dreams. Where else, they reason, can one live in such harmony with nature — a philosophy that is a way of life for the in habitants of Marin County, the far North, as well as the beach and desert communities of central and southern California, including San Diego. As a result, real estate prices are extremely high in comparison to the rest of the country.

Surfing and miles of beach have been forever identified with California in the nation's mind, and that of the world.

City dwellers are accustomed to traveling long distances in a short amount of time on the weekend to get away from the traffic and unwind in the pristine surroundings of Lake Tahoe or Yosemite National Park. Fitness, health and recreation, a credo shared by all groups, is expressed by mountain biking, surfing, kayaking, skiing and water-skiing, hiking, sailing etc.

Californians are very vocal about preserving the state's great natural beauty. At the moment, developers have a hard time going ahead with their projects, since in many cases it has become time-consuming and difficult to get what they want done. Ultra-left protectionists advocate NIMBY,

development anywhere but "not in my backyard." Even George Lucas was stopped in his tracks when trying to make some of his dreams a reality in Marin County.

Generalities often hold a grain of truth, such as the one that Californians are individualists and independent thinkers, people with high standards, who create their own destiny. Twentysomethings move away from home at college time, choose a career to please themselves, not their parents, and seldom, if ever, move back to their home town. Ideological and political beliefs are strongly felt, and part of the somewhat fanatical California character. "If something feels right, you fight," says one Santa Barbara native, "with demonstrations, placards and all the rest. This is supposed to be Utopia, after all, the freest place in which you can live. This freedom allows you to have the opinions you want, and to express them." Hence California was the birthplace of the 1950s beat generation, the Free Speech movement and the Summer of Love in the 1960s, the breeding ground of both avant-garde trends and ultra-right politics often adopted at a later date by the rest of the country, and the world. These ideas, coupled with the state's productive farmland, have inspired unimpressed out-of-staters to label California as "the land of fruit and nuts."

Californians live in an open territory seldom encumbered by the harsh climatic conditions of winter, and it is thought that these ideal conditions contribute to their open, extroverted personalities. Even the introspection of spiritual seeking, a current mode, is often done in a gregarious group atmosphere.

Looking good and feeling good is part of California's credo. Below, fitness freaks provide local color in Venice.

A word about Southern California: reality is surprisingly like the movies and the T.V. sitcoms filmed there. Muscle Beach actually exists, as do beautiful people who strut their stuff, so to speak. If life in California is on the cutting edge, the fine line between fantasy and every day's needs can be blurred at times in Southern California. If the natives of California like to think of themselves as a highly-accomplished population, then Southern Californians work hard at almost everything, whether it be looking good, having a great tan, a fit body, a super car or earning professional recognition in the eyes of their peers, and the world. In comparison to the rest of the state, many things appear to be magnified in Southern California. There seem to be an impossible number of traffic lanes clogged up by an impossible number of cars in and around L.A., plus, in the eyes of an Easterner (non-Californian), thanks to a rust-free environment, an incredible amount of perfectly preserved, pricey vintage cars. The 3,500,000 residents of Los Angeles lead frenetic lives under a blanket of smog, while a short distance down the coast, the tenets of a pleasant, turn-of-the-century beach community are codified in the tranquil surroundings of San Diego.

Besides mobility, another thing ubiquitous to the entire state is the concept of "California cuisine," a blend of European, Asian and African culinary traditions concocted with only the freshest of native-grown ingredients. And if the glitter of the Golden State has tarnished in recent years, Californians are ready to pick up and move to secondary Utopias, such as Washington State, Oregon and Montana, and thousands of would-be Californians are eager to take their place.

California has something for everyone: from snowcapped mountains to pristine beaches, from spectacular deserts to vineyards that produce world-famous wines. And, California is truly a sportsman's paradise. The resident and the visitor alike can choose to walk in the beauty of a redwood forest, go skiing at Lake Tahoe, be a beach bum all along the coast, play golf on any of the many well-tended greens, do some strenuous hiking in Yosemite Park or go mountain biking in Marin County.

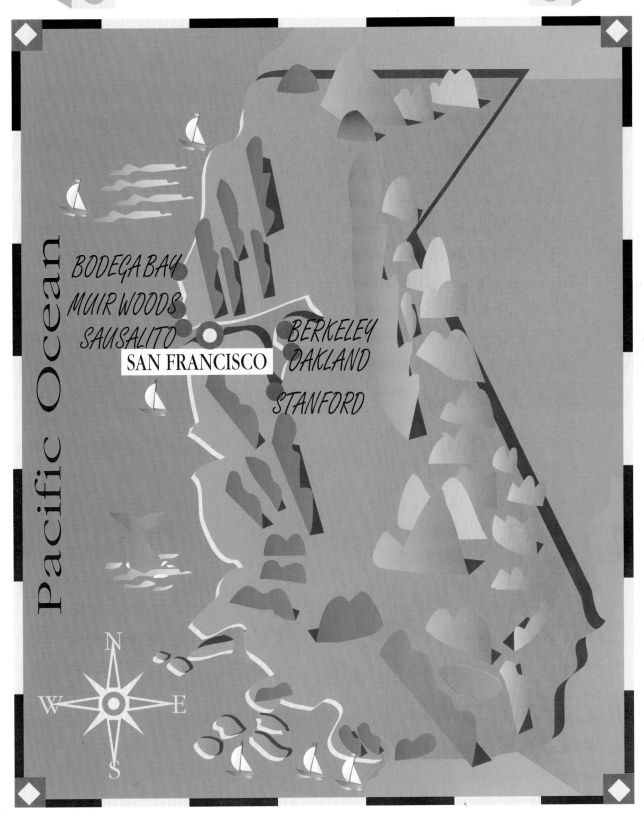

Pacific Ocean

BODEGA BAY
MUIR WOODS
SAUSALITO
SAN FRANCISCO
BERKELEY
OAKLAND
STANFORD

# SAN FRANCISCO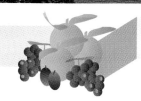

San Francisco's unique character and great beauty come from its position on a narrow peninsula nearly surrounded by water. Five thousand miles away from Tokyo across the Pacific, the city overlooks the ocean, and dominates the San Francisco Bay. One can smell the salt air in San Francisco and feel the energy of the sea. The vibrant light shimmers against the city's forty-odd hills, covered in green parks, wide streets and bright buildings.

One of San Francisco's outstanding landmarks is, of course, the poetic **Golden Gate Bridge.** The name "Golden Gate" refers both to a natural and a man-made wonder. In 1848, explorer John C. Fremont so christened the narrow straits between the Pacific Ocean and the San Francisco Bay in his *Geographical Memoir of California.* The Golden Gate Bridge, on the other hand, which connects the city to Marin County, was opened to traffic in May 1937. It was built to withstand gales as well as strong currents, and its central section rises 260 feet above the water to allow Navy battleships to pass under if necessary. Some 100,000 cars cross it every day. When the fog rolls in, as it often does, only the 746-foot towers remain visible above the mist.

Nearby is the **Golden Gate Park,** where sand dunes were transformed into a verdant garden between 1890 and 1943 by the intrepid John McLaren. McLaren personally planted grass, flowers and trees, including redwoods, in order to create a green setting where nearly every imaginable sport can be practiced. Especially popular with visitors are such attractions as the **Japanese Tea Garden,** the **Conservatory of Flowers,** an intricate Victorian greenhouse made in Dublin and shipped to San Francisco around Cape Horn, and the **M.H. de Young Memorial Museum.** The museum chronicles Western art from antiquity up to the 20th century, and a wing of the same building houses the **Asian Art Museum.**

*Above, at 4,200 ft. in length, the **Golden Gate Bridge** is one of the longest suspension bridges in the world. It is open to pedestrians as well as cars.*

*Next page, on a clear day, you can see the **Golden Gate Bridge** spanning San Francisco Bay over to Marin county; on a foggy day, while all else is hidden, the bridge remains above the mist. Page 13: San Francisco's **financial district.** One of the most prominent skyscrapers (far left) is the **Transamerica Pyramid**; an unexpected surprise is the redwood grove at its base.*

On a more prosaic note, much of the Pacific coast, along with a steady proportion of world commerce, hums to the rhythms of San Francisco's **Financial District** (pictured on page 13), which had its origins in the Gold Rush of 1849 and was built on...a landfill!

The Gold Rush started in a modest way. A New Jersey carpenter, James Marshall, found a nugget of gold outside San Francisco while constructing a sawmill on property belonging to John Sutter. The word spread like wildfire, and the population of the town exploded overnight. The boom was on.

Gold diggers arrived by boat at Yerba Buena Cove. Eventually, the cove's mud flats and the area up to the sea wall were filled with sand as well as soil from some of the city's smaller hills. This is where the first banking offices were set up in the 1850s and '60s to handle the assets of the Gold Rush and of silver from Nevada's Comstock Lode.

Perhaps San Francisco's most famous banker was A.P. Giannini, who opened the Bank of Italy at the turn of the century. During the earthquake of 1906, Giannini hid the bank's deposits in a fruit and vegetable wagon, and was one of the first banking officials to honor withdrawals from customers after the disaster. The Bank of Italy eventually turned into the **Bank of America;** its corporate headquarters in San Francisco are located in a 52-story carnelian red marble skyscraper. The building which stands out among the tall silhouettes which house insurance, corporate and international banking offices is the famous **Transamerica Pyramid.** Designed by a Los Angeles firm, the Pyramid has turned into a symbol of San Francisco, much to the chagrin of the natives.

East of the Financial District is the spectacular complex known as the **Embarcadero Center.** Its pillars are four skyscrapers plus a Hyatt Regency hotel, all connected above street level by pedestrian walkways. Another outstanding feature of the Embarcedero Center is a variety of outdoor sculptures; the **Vaillancourt Fountain,** a sort of urban Stonehenge, is probably the most well-known of the group.

11

*Go up **Twin Peaks Boulevard** all the way up to the top for a splendid panorama of downtown San Francisco and a glimpse of the **San Francisco-Oakland Bay Bridge** (in the background).*

The best vista of San Francisco can be had from the summit of the city's second and third highest hills - **Twin Peaks.** The 360° panorama is spectacular, to say the least. And in the distance one can catch a glimpse of the **San Francisco-Oakland Bay Bridge** (above) which from this height appears to be a silvery-gold ribbon. It is the world's longest steel bridge and an impressive sight.

Everyone who comes to San Francisco wants to know about the famous earthquake which took place on April 18, 1906. The shock, measuring 8.3 on the Richter scale, jolted San Franciscans out of bed before breakfast. The aftermath was devastating. Fires burned out of control for three days due to broken water mains, and entire city blocks had to be dynamited to check their spread. In the end, some 50,000 buildings were destroyed, and there were over 500 casualties.

San Franciscans re-constructed their city with their usual indomitable spirit. A number of **Victorian houses** (following page), precious city landmarks,

remained standing, while the others were later rebuilt. A tribute to carpentry art, row upon row of these famed houses were erected during the late 1800s in four basic styles: Queen Anne, Stick, Italianate and Georgian. Elements in an individual house may include gable and turret roofs, deep recesses and bay windows, stained glass, Ionic, Corinthian and plain columns, ornately carved pediments, wooden filigree and deep porches, all painted in strong, clear colors with white trim. Due to the interweaving of various influences, the architectural style can only be called San Franciscan.

The 1906 earthquake also buried the old City Hall, clearing the way for a bold, large-scale architectural complex known as the **Civic Center,** a group of expressly-designed federal, state and city buildings in the Beaux-Arts style. The project was envisaged by city planner Daniel Burnham and carried forward after his death by architect Arthur Brown Jr., who studied at Paris's Ecole des Beaux-Art. The new **City Hall** is a model of grandeur, topped by a dome taller than that of the U.S. Capitol. The Beaux-Art design extends to other nearby structures, including the **War Memorial Opera House,** where representatives from 50 countries signed the United Nations founding charter in 1945. The War Memorial Opera House, Davies Hall, the War Memorial Veterans Building and the Ballet Building are united under the single title of the **San Francisco War Memorial and Performing Arts Center,** which also houses the **San Francisco Museum of Modern Art.** This fine collection includes works by Henri Matisse, Paul Klee and Jackson Pollock among others. Always on a modern note, the Civic Center's most recent addition (1980), the **Louise M. Davies Symphony Hall**, breaks the general Beaux-Arts theme with a contemporary glass design. The San Francisco Symphony holds concerts there from October to May.

The downtown area is also a mecca for shoppers. It is filled with antique and jewelry shops, art galleries, small boutiques and large department stores. The heart of the district is **Union Square,** a 2.6 acre park resplendent with palm and yew trees, box hedges, flowers as well as stone benches. The surroundings do not speak of war, yet a statue of Victory atop a granite column commemorates Admiral Dewey's triumph at Manila Bay during the Spanish-American War. And the square itself, presented to the city in 1850 by Mayor Geary, received its name from several pro-Union rallies held there during the Civil War.

Today, Union Square is home to flower vendors (part of the local scene since the early 1900s), street artists, musicians and flocks of pigeons. The square is set over an enormous underground parking garage, handy for shoppers, many of whom head for **Maiden Lane,** a street lined with exclusive boutiques. One would never guess that until the earthquake it was called Morton Street, famed for its bawdy houses. In this case, destruction meant a new name and new life.

*San Francisco's **Victorian homes,** also known as **"The Painted Ladies,"** are a favorite with tourists and residents alike. The Pacific Heights area in particular contains many such homes, a tribute to the 19th century carpenter's art.*

Left, the **cable car** is an easy way of going up and down the city's hills. This one is climbing Hyde Street from Fisherman's Wharf.

Above, **Alcatraz** last made the headlines during the 1970s when the island was occupied by a group of Native Americans. Today, it is a top tourist attraction in the Bay Area.

Clang, clang, here comes a San Francisco **cable car**! This local institution was invented by Andrew Hallidie, who was at the controls during the inaugural ride up Nob Hill on August 1, 1873. An immediate success, the San Francisco cable car system expanded to include 600 operating cars, more than eight lines and 110 miles of track. The earthquake destroyed much of this network, which was never rebuilt. Yet the cable car, an essential part of San Francisco life, was declared a National Historic Landmark in 1964 and continues to operate.

Three lines exist today: the Powell-Hyde, the Powell-Mason and the California, with a total of 37 cars running on 10 miles of track. The ride is a steady 9 1/2 miles an hour, with the continuously-winding cable below street level. With no built-in reverse, cable cars have to be manually turned around at the end of the line.

The fun of a cable car ride provides a vivid contrast to an ominous-looking island in the background: **Alcatraz** (above). Though not in use as a federal penitentiary since 1963, the name is still enough to send chills down one's spine. The 12 acres comprising the island are pure stone, hence the nickname ''The Rock;'' currents around it are strong and the water freezing cold. It was presumed that no one could ever escape.

Alcatraz's past has always been a grim one. Originally the site of a U.S. Army prison during the Civil War, Alcatraz was later turned into a maximum security prison in 1934, at the height of the gangster era. Al Capone, Pretty Boy Floyd and of course the ''Birdman of Alcatraz'' were locked up in cells converted from military use.

It is now a protected wildlife refuge, bringing to mind the day in 1775 when Lieutenant Juan Manuel de Ayala christened the Rock **Isla de los Alcatraces** (Island of the Pelicans). But it has always been a lonely spot. Perhaps there could be no greater punishment in the world than viewing the entire city of San Francisco, so vividly alive, from behind prison bars.

The **San Francisco-Oakland Bay Bridge,** *also known simply as the Bay Bridge, connects the Financial District to the city of Oakland.*

The feisty Dungeness crab is the logo of **Fisherman's Wharf,** and rightly so. Fresh seafood is what counts here: crab, along with shrimp, abalone, squid, sea bass, salmon, mackerel and cod. This is what lures a small fleet of fishermen, many of whom are of Italian origin, to sail out from Fisherman's Wharf every morning at 3 am. When they return in the afternoon, there is often a crowd of onlookers to see what the catch of the day is. The colorful proceedings are augmented by the presence of vendors who serve steamed, cracked crabs out of cauldrons, along with other fish specialties. For a pleasant evening out, the area is also lined with fine seafood restaurants. While Fisherman's Wharf has gotten somewhat touristy in recent years as souvenir shops, craft stands and other commercial attractions have moved there, a certain atmosphere remains alive as you watch the fishermen tie up their boats. Something else to watch is the blessing of the fleet, which takes place in early October. These same ships herald the arrival of every New Year by blowing their whistles precisely at midnight.

The harbor is also home to a number of historic craft open to tours. One such ship is the **Balclutha**, an old three-masted square rigger. Built in Scotland in 1883, the Balclutha sailed around Cape Horn many times to bring staples and luxury goods from Europe to San Francisco. As a floating museum, the Balclutha is a reminder of a glorious past.

On the rest of the San Francisco waterfront, smart developers have successfully converted reminders of an industrial past into profitable and enjoyable marketplaces. The outstanding example is, of course, **Ghirardelli Square.** This red brick structure was the site of a woolen works until an Italian immigrant, Domenico Ghiradelli, turned it into a chocolate factory. In the 1960s it was completely renovated so that the original premises could host modern and often whimsical shops, restaurants, cafés, theaters and exhibitions. The fairytale atmosphere is heightened by a clock tower

Fisherman's Wharf is the place to go for take-away seafood or a seafood dinner with all the trimmings. The fishing boats go out before dawn and come back with their catch of the day.

illuminated at night, which overlooks strolling mimes, street musicians and jugglers who provide on-the-spot entertainment. And huge bars of Ghirardelli chocolate, now made elsewhere, are still for sale.

The same formula was used in restoring the **Cannery,** an old Del Monte peach canning establishment which dated back to 1909. It is now a complex containing shops and restaurants; an especially attractive feature is the outdoor concerts set in a courtyard shaded by century-old olive trees.

Back to the water's edge, yet another entertainment/shopping/eating experience can be found in **Pier 39,** built of weathered timber from demolished piers. A colorful Venetian carrousel is the highlight of a mini-amusement park, and there are over 100 shops in which to browse. Pier 39 is also flanked by two marinas where numerous boats are docked. Some of the fleet anchored here provide short and long sightseeing cruises of San Francisco Bay.

Above, **Chinatown** offers a living impression of life in the Orient as it once was.

Left, **Lombard Street** on Russian Hill advertises itself as "the crookedest street in the world."

First and foremost, San Francisco is a city of hills: **Nob Hill,** former home of the "nabobs," Gold Rush and railroad barons, now an extremely elegant residential area, and **Telegraph Hill** (284 feet), where the first telegraph station in the West (1853) was placed. This area is now a sort of Greenwich Village, home to artists and writers who live in frame houses and apartment buildings often perched on rocky inclines. Telegraph Hill's outstanding landmark is the **Coit Tower,** which resembles a fire-hose nozzle. The money used to build the Tower was a bequest from San Francisco eccentric Lillie Hitchcock Coit, a fan of firefighters and honorary member of Knickerbocker Engine Company 5.

No less famous than Telegraph Hill is **Russian Hill,** which derived its name from the fact that a section was used as a burial ground for Russian sailors. Writers and intellectuals have been traditionally drawn to Russian Hill, known for its sweeping vistas, steep paths, open green spaces and innovative architecture.

The much-photographed **Lombard Street** (left), is found on Russian Hill. Lombard Street's amazing hairpin curves are carefully landscaped with bushes and flowers, making a ride down it an esthetic experience as well as a trip to satisfy one's sense of adventure.

San Francisco is also synonymous with **Chinatown.** The ceremonial gateway to Chinatown is more than merely symbolic, for one enters another world, that of the largest Chinese enclave outside Asia. The immediate impression is one of myriad colors and crowdedness: the reds, greens, oranges and yellows of banners, signs and pagoda roofs overlook premises jammed with trinkets and treasures of ivory, jade, cloisonné, porcelain and teak. Needless to say, dining in Chinatown is an experience not to be missed, and the Chinese New Year, which takes place either in February or early March, is an event to mark on everyone's calendar. The celebration lasts a full week, spilling over to every street in Chinatown.

*The non-denominational **Memorial Church,** replete with arches, a rose window and turrets, is a symbol of **Stanford University.***

STANFORD

South of San Francisco, the once-sleepy suburbs along the coast and the farmland in the Santa Clara Valley has been transformed into the high-tech and prosperous **Silicon Valley,** which has the highest number of electronic firms per square mile in the entire country. The name derives from the manufacture of silicon chips, a multimillion-dollar business. Converted into the vital parts of computers, military and space communications devices and even something as mundane as the microwave oven, the thin wafer has been responsible for many of our technological advances.

Also located in the Silicon Valley is **Palo Alto,** literally "Tall Tree". This is how Spanish explorers referred to the area thanks to a centuries'-old redwood which now marks the city's northwestern entrance. The surroundings furnish no clue that the visitor to the city can trace the thirty year-plus career of a child's toy favorite in the Barbie Doll Hall of Fame. More importantly, Palo Alto is also home to the Hewlett-Packard company, as well as Stanford University, best known for its medical, law and engineering schools.

Looking at **Stanford University** today, it's hard to believe that this institute of higher learning was founded on the site of a former horse ranch. Leland Stanford's proposal to start a university in the West on family property in memory of his dead son provoked derisive comment from Eastern academicians. But the railroad magnate went ahead, little dreaming that Nobel laureates and Pulitzer

Prize winners would eventually be faculty members, and that research conducted here would pave the way for heart transplants, the Pill, microprocessors, IQ tests and genetic engineering. Most of this activity goes on behind closed doors, although a tour is available of both the medical school and the **Stanford Linear Accelerator Center,** where the speed of charged sub-atomic particles is increased by radio-frequency electric fields in a two-mile-long vacuum tube. Particle physics, the study of the fundamental components of matter and the forces between them, involves the use of this type of machine in order to force particles close enough together to produce interactions.

Experimentation of a different sort was carried out by Stanford fellow Ken Kesey, who earned the money necessary to his survival by administering test drugs to mentally ill hospital patients. He also supported himself by working as an orderly in a psychiatric ward, and both experiences inspired the book *One Flew Over the Cuckoo's Nest.*

Clusters of sandstone buildings, topped by red-tiled roofs, give the 8,200 acre campus a peaceful Spanish mission look. The architect responsible for integrating the college buildings into a natural setting was Frederick Law Olmstead, the planner of

Central Park. One landmark, however, the **Memorial Church,** is a little more elaborate. The edifice, richly decorated with murals and stained glass in a style that is a cross between Romanesque and Moorish, is the outstanding feature of the **Inner Quad.** Not far away, the **Hoover Tower** signals the visitor's arrival to the **Hoover Institution on War, Revolution and Peace,** containing millions of documents pertinent to the First World War. Hoover, one of the first graduates of Stanford, had organized relief efforts to help the destitute at the end of the far-reaching conflict. On the literary side, the **Charles D. Field Collection of Ernest Hemingway** in the Stanford Library contains the author's manuscripts both in published and unpublished form, including rare first editions. Art is not neglected either, as is clearly demonstrated by a tour of the **Leland Stanford Jr. Museum,** known for its exhibitions of Egyptian and Oriental artifacts, paintings and sculptures. And, the justly famous **Rodin Sculpture Garden** boasts the most complete collection of the artist's work outside Paris, comprising original castings of *The Burghers of Calais* and *The Kiss.* The beauty of nature can be appreciated at the **Bayland's Nature Reserve,** a place to enjoy hiking and birdwatching.

Stanford University boasts a beautiful natural setting for its nearly 7,000 students. Right, *the campus's* **Hoover Tower.**

*A birds-eye view of **U.C. Berkeley;** in the foreground, Memorial Stadium; in the background, the distinctive **Sather Tower** or **Campanile**, a replica of the Venetian bell tower in St. Mark's Square.*

BERKELEY

University of California, revolution, book shops, California cuisine are the words that come most often to mind when thinking about Berkeley.

Berkeley has been a college town since the founding of the first of nine University of California campuses here shortly after the Civil War. Later christened in honor of George Berkeley, an 18th century Anglican bishop and philosopher, U.C. Berkeley became a reality thanks to the staunch efforts of the Reverend Henry Durant.

Only one original building from Durant's time is left, **South Hall,** a red-brick presence that stands in the shadow of much-photographed **Sather Tower,** better known as the **Campanile.** The monument is a 1914 facsimile of the quintessential Venetian bell tower *(campanile)* in St. Mark's Square. The *Campanile's* 61 bells are rung punctually at 7:50 am, 12 noon and 6 pm, and visitors can ride to the top of the 307-ft. tower to admire a bird's-eye view of the surrounding area.

Other notable sights include the **University Art Museum,** home to works by Cezanne, Picasso, Francis Bacon and Hans Hoffman, and the **Lawrence Hall of Science,** an outstanding museum that features many hands-on exhibits. Close by are the **Memorial Stadium** and the carefully landscaped **Botanical Gardens,** an Eden of rhododendrons, cacti and other plants.

Revolution arrived in Berkeley during the 1960s thanks to a campus directive which placed restrictions on political activity. The outcome was the Free Speech Movement, and demonstrations against the war in Vietnam were the order of the day. The battle to save People's Park (1969) came about when students protested the university's expansion into the nearby city.

As could be expected, book shops abound in downtown Berkeley, which has also become a hotbed of gastronomic innovation. Starting in the 1970s, local restaurateurs began using strictly fresh local (and often gourmet) ingredients when preparing time-honored European recipes. The result is ubiquitous "California cuisine."

OAKLAND

Across the Bay from San Francisco and just south of Berkeley lies **Oakland,** home of the champion Oakland A's baseball team and an important transportation hub. An impressive sight is the **Bay Bridge,** a silvery span connecting San Francisco to Oakland and the world's longest steel bridge. Many travelers to northern California find the **Oakland International Airport** a viable alternative to its San Francisco counterpart, and the Port of Oakland handles such a massive amount of commercial shipping that it ranks as one of the world's major container ports.

As could be imagined from its strategic position, Oakland is predominantly an industrial city, a far cry from the Spanish colonial period when the land was dotted with oak trees. The **Tribune Tower** (1923), a fairytale-like skyscraper and headquarters of the *Oakland Tribune* newspaper, is a distinctive landmark.

Oakland is also the unlikely birthplace of literary figures Gertrude Stein and Jack London. Stein was not in the least kind to Oakland in her memoirs *(there is no there there);* while Jack London, a vagrant sailor, preferred to concentrate on the beauty of the Alaskan wilderness *(The Call of the Wild).* The result is amusing: "there" is used in many of the city's slogans to contradict Stein's philosophy, and a group of restaurants and shops along the waterfront catering to the tourist trade has been renamed **Jack London Square.**

Oakland is centered around water even away from the coast. The city's major park is near **Lake Merritt,** which had an outlet into the Bay until it was dammed up in the late 1860s. Here, one can relax, practice a sport or take a cruise on a replica of a Mississippi riverboat. Lake Merritt is but a stone's throw from the **Oakland Museum.** Covering a wide range of subjects, the museum offers something of interest for everyone: modern art, turn-of-the-century furniture, vintage photography, artifacts pertaining to the history of California and a display of Bay Area habitats.

The **Oakland** skyline. *The city of Berkeley and U.C. Berkeley (left) borders the city.*

***Sausalito** is a quick and pleasant getaway from San Francisco; besides the town's scenic beauty, the weekend flea market is also popular. Above, characteristic **houseboats** fill the harbor.*

MARIN COUNTY

The Golden Gate Bridge is *the* gateway to Marin County, a Nirvana to its wealthy inhabitants, many of whom are attuned to the natural beauty of their surroundings and a holistic lifestyle. There is much more to Marin, however, than hot tubs and mountain bikes (despite the fact that the latter were invented here). The territory, comprising rocky cliffs, coastal brush, redwood and evergreen forests, chaparral, meadows, salt-water lagoons, swamps and sandy beaches, is loosely divided into East and West Marin.

East Marin

A favorite pastime of San Franciscans is to have Sunday brunch in **Sausalito**, a former fishing village accessible by car or ferry. Sausalito has gone upscale in terms of restaurants and boutiques, but a glimpse of its original charm is still visible in the many picturesque **houseboats** docked in the harbor. Interesting to visit is the **Bay Model Museum,** a working simulation of powerful tides and currents underlying San Francisco Bay. North of Sausalito, **Mill Valley,** as can be imagined from its name, once prepared the lumber to be used in the building of San Francisco's characteristic Victorian houses. The town lies on the eastern slope of **Mount Tamalpais,** affectionately known as "Mount Tam" or "The Sleeping Maiden" because of its curving landscape. Marin County's highest hill is part of a spectacular natural park perfect for hikes and nature walks. The view from the top encompasses San Francisco to the south and cliffs and unspoiled shoreline to the west.

There are few sights more beautiful than the **Muir Woods** in the morning after a rainstorm. The mist clings to the ferns and underbrush carpeting the redwood forest, and the sunlight filters down from the tops of the trees. The coastal redwoods, once widespread in North America, are confined to but a few spots now, and the Muir Woods, comprising an area of 300 acres, was declared a national monument by President Theodore Roosevelt in order to safeguard the species. The majestic trees can reach a height of 300 feet, and the trunks often measure from 10 to 15 feet in diameter. The reserve, great for nature walks, was named after naturalist John Muir by the actual benefactor, William Kent. A native of Scotland, Muir had spent time in the Yosemite Valley and around Mount Shasta, and was impressed by their beauty. He urged that the areas be protected, and thus helped to create the national park system.

San Rafael is the Marin County seat, and Frank Lloyd Wright designed the government buildings — his last project — that constitute the **Marin Civic Center.** Otherwise, one might recognize some of the scenery which acted as a backdrop for the movie *American Graffiti.* In the immediate vicinity, the antique shops of **San Anselmo** draw a weekend crowd of tourists and native Californians alike.

West Marin

Mainly off-limits to cars, the **Golden Gate National Recreation Area** is a wonderful natural playground that stretches from the end of the Golden Gate Bridge to the beginning of the Point Reyes National Seashore. The first stop are the **Marin Headlands,** a favorite place for birdwatching. The rocky promontories make for dramatic and mainly unspoiled scenery, with the exception of...discarded military barracks and weapon sites! The headlands' strategic location with regards to San Francisco made a natural site for artillery batteries and other installations from the Civil War right up to the 1950s. For instance, Kirby Beach is located below remnants of Spanish-American War fortifications, and the **Visitor's Center** is next to a discarded missile launching pad. A contrast to all of this is the **Marine Mammal Center,** where injured sea animals recuperate under the care of an expert staff before returning to their original habitats. The extremity of the Marin Headlands is illuminated by the **Point Bonita Lighthouse.**

Further along the coast are **Muir Beach** and **Stinson Beach,** popular with sunbathers and fishermen, a decided contrast to **Bolinas,** where the inhabitants want to keep the nonresidents out so badly that they have removed all the signs leading to this picturesque village. Another nature preserve is found at the **Bolinas Lagoon,**

The **Muir Woods,** *domain of the beautiful coastal redwood tree, was one of the first areas in the country to be set aside as a natural reserve.*

abounding in birdlife and sea creatures.

The **Point Reyes National Seashore** is the western rim of a peninsula delineated by the Tomales Bay and the San Andreas Fault. The area, originally located down by Los Angeles, continues to float in a northwesterly direction at the rate of two inches or so every year. **Earthquake Trail** attracts tourists wanting to see the stone fence which moved 15 feet during the 1906 San Francisco earthquake. To the delight of nature lovers, on "terra ferma" the Point Reyes seashore is characterized by tide pools, beaches, strong currents, hiking trails, ridges dotted with wildflowers, and lookouts for whale watching. Sir Francis Drake is thought to have explored Point Reyes during his travels in the late 1500s, and his name is given to a bay here.

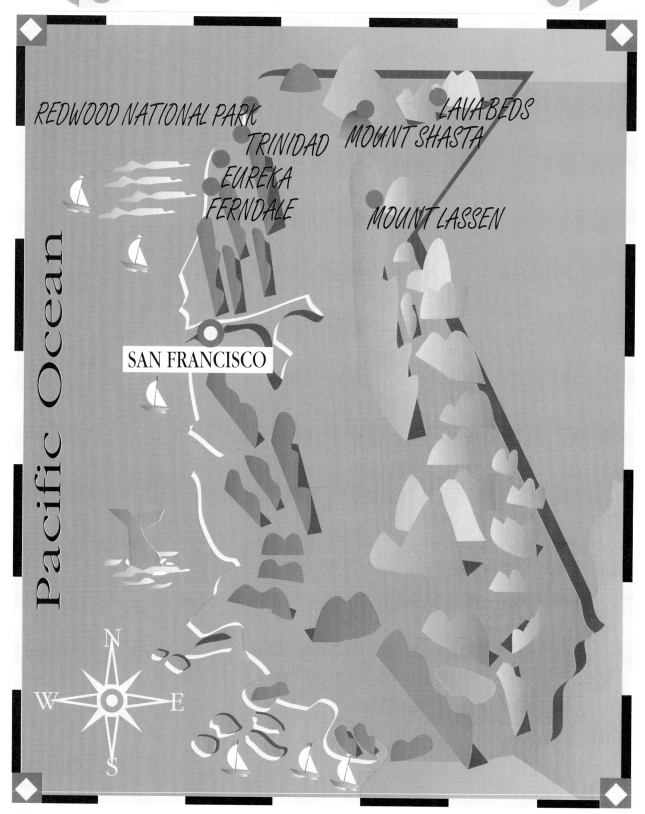

REDWOOD NATIONAL PARK

TRINIDAD

EUREKA

FERNDALE

LAVA BEDS

MOUNT SHASTA

MOUNT LASSEN

Pacific Ocean

SAN FRANCISCO

N
W   E
S

Eureka is one place to start a tour of California's North Coast. Unlike the rest of California, Eureka was settled not by the Spanish, but by the Russians in search of furs, followed by the Americans. Victorian homes are a precious town legacy from the nineteenth century.

EUREKA

"Eureka!" (I have found it!) cried James T. Ryan when he discovered what was later to be called the **Humboldt Bay** in 1850. The whale hunter was ecstatic at finding a large natural bay along the predominantly rocky **North Coast,** which stretches from the present Bodega Bay up to the Redwood National Park. Ryan, however, was not the first white man to set foot in the area; that honor is reserved to several anonymous Russian seal hunters early in the century, followed by Josiah Gregg in 1849, who arrived from inland with an expedition. The inlet's name commemorates the exploits of German naturalist and geographer Alexander von Humboldt (1769-1859), who spent many years exploring central Asia and South America.

For those who have time, the proper way to take in the sights of the North Coast is to begin at its southern point, **Bodega Bay,** then slowly drive to Eureka and Arcata via the Sonoma Coast, Mendocino and the Lost Coast. Bodega Bay is famed for its annual **Fisherman's Festival** which takes place in April, and antique shops which attract aficionados from all over the state. A few miles inland is **Bodega,** which Alfred Hitchcock used as a setting for *The Birds.* Most of the buildings in the movie are still standing, a fact that the natives of Bodega prefer to downplay. Back to the coast, the Russian River flows into the sea at **Jenner,** a haven for seals and otters, and most of the coast between Bodega Bay and Jenner comprises the **Sonoma Coast State Beaches,** protected from development, and perfect for fishing and sunbathing along the sandy coves tucked into the base of rocky cliffs. Swimming is discouraged, however, as the waves are high, the water cold, and the undercurrent quite strong.

While Bodega Bay was christened by Spanish

explorer Don Juan Francisco de la Bodega, the first settlers of the area were probably Russian trappers from Alaska in search of seal and sea otter pelts. After driving the marine mammals close to extinction, the Russians departed the territory for good during the 1840s. They were to leave visible traces of their presence north of Jenner at **Fort Ross,** a military outpost which John Sutter purchased two years before gold was discovered on his property near San Francisco. Time has not been kind to the settlement: the Russian Orthodox church was leveled by the 1906 earthquake, although it was later reconstructed, and the only original buildings left are the officers' barracks. There is also an interesting museum which provides insight into the Russians' way of life and exhibits of Pomo (local Native American) craftsmanship.

Further up, one can camp at the **Salt Point State Park,** and catch a glimpse of remarkable sandstone formations caused by erosion. Then wander among the towering plants of the **Kruse Rhododendron Reserve,** especially if it's springtime.

The sea cliffs become steeper and the shore rocks more precarious along the **Mendocino Headlands Park.** The town of **Mendocino,** charming and decidedly un-California-like in the traditional sense, features a lovely bay view and turn-of-the century frame houses built in an markedly Eastern style. James Dean put Mendocino on the map in the 1950s thanks to *East of Eden,* and an artist's colony subsequently reinforced the town's fame. Many of the original group left to seek their fortunes elsewhere, but their legacy has lingered in the **Mendocino Art Center,** also home to displays of photography and craftsmanship.

A contrast to the poetry of Mendocino is the prosaic **Fort Bragg,** not to be confused with the military post of the same name located in North Carolina. The North Coast's Fort Bragg, founded in the 1850s, was meant to defend settlers from attacks by Native Americans, but it was soon abandoned and its later residents turned their attention to the abundant forest resources. Many continue to work in the lumber mills, or to turn their hand to fishing. A remainder of the old days can be experienced by riding the **Skunk Train,** a California Western steam train 40 miles from Fort Bragg to the unexciting town of Willits. Once used for trade and commerce, the

*Don't miss out on a **seafood dinner** when visiting **Eureka,** since fishing continues to be a major industry here.*

*The **Eureka harbor** is home to pleasure craft as well as the fishing fleet. While here, take time out for a cruise of the North Coast.*

Skunk Train (a sweeter smelling replica of the original, so-called because of the locomotive's smelly fumes) now provides scenic rides through redwood groves, and the promise of cold beer or other refreshments at journey's end.

Blocked by the King Mountain Range, Highway One swings inland north of Fort Bragg, so Nature triumphs along the rugged **Lost Coast,** accessible to boaters and hikers and to cars only via secondary (often dirt) roads. The Lost Coast signals one's arrival in **Humboldt County,** only a short ride away from the **Humboldt Redwoods State Park,** and Eureka.

Fittingly, **Eureka** and its port were founded to serve the needs of Gold Rush towns in the interior. Unlike other places, Eureka did not become a ghost town once the Gold Rush went bust; it is the largest settlement (pop. 25,000) on the California coast north of San Francisco.

What remains of Eureka's glory days is a goodly number of **Victorian houses,** located in the **Old**

Town. Chief among these is the magnificent **Carson Mansion** (pictured on page 32), built in 1885 by William Carson and now the site of a private men's club. Carson made his money in redwood lumber, as did (and do) many of Eureka's inhabitants. The turrets and slanting roofs of this gingerbread masterpiece were designed with the area's high rainfall average in mind. Facing the mansion is the so-called **Pink Lady,** another intricately carved structure resplendent with stained glass. A pleasant way to spend an afternoon is to go on the driving tour of the Victorian homes sponsored by Eureka's Chamber of Commerce.

Another stop-off is the **Clarke Museum,** a treasury of Native American artifacts that includes an outstanding collection of baskets in addition to antique arms, crafts and toys belonging to the first Eureka settlers. Retired high school teacher Cecile Clarke dedicated his retirement years to putting together the impressive collection, which first went on public view in 1960. That wood is and continues

to be important to both the local economy and art can be seen in the **Roman Gabriel Sculpture Garden,** containing imaginative depictions of famous and unknown people and plants. The folk art created by Gabriel has received international recognition.

The area's local Pacific Ocean heritage is explained in detail at the **Humboldt Bay Maritime Museum.** Eureka is also an excellent place for a good fish dinner, as salmon, rainbow trout and other seafood delicacies abound in the North Coast. But the lumberjacks of old had heartier appetites, as attested by the nearby **Somoa Cookhouse,** across the Somoa bridge. As could be expected, diners are served huge helpings of meat and potatoes in the last old-time cookhouse in the West. Otherwise, explore the **dunes** in Somoa, or take a ride up to Arcata and visit the **Humboldt State University** and the **Arcata Marsh and Wildlife Sanctuary.**

*The gingerbread fantasy-like **Carson Mansion** can only be admired from the outside since it is presently the headquarters of an all-men's private club. The mansion was built in the 1880s by a lumber magnate.*

*Above: Victorian **homes** are yet again a chief characteristic of the North Coast town of **Ferndale**. Right: **Trinidad** maintains its maritime tradition even today.*

FERNDALE

Eureka's immediate environs offer pleasant day trips to two villages of note, Ferndale and Trinidad. Ferndale boasts a number of exquisitely-preserved Victorian homes; chief among these is the whimsical **Gingerbread Mansion** (above) complete with a carefully landscaped garden. If the Gingerbread Mansion happens to be the house of your dreams, then make a reservation to spend the night: this Ferndale landmark has been turned into a comfortable bed-and-breakfast inn. The town's architecture sets the tone for the month-long **Victorian Christmas,** sure to delight children of all ages. The highlights of the celebration include a tall, old-fashioned Christmas tree, and visits by both Saint Nicholas and Santa Claus. Surprisingly enough, Ferndale was the nucleus of a Danish community during the Civil War, but the seafaring Portuguese were soon to follow. The **Holy Ghost Festival,** which takes place in May, has its roots in the Portuguese tradition. And, to get a taste of the Lost Coast scenery, head to **Ross Park.**

TRINIDAD

The village's vaguely Caribbean name comes from the fact that its natural port was discovered by Spanish explorers on the feast of the Holy Trinity. Settled in 1850 as the North Coast's oldest outpost, **Trinidad** later became a minor whaling center, until the stock was depleted at the turn of the century. Salmon fishing continues to contribute an important part of the town's economy, and tourism also thrives thanks to the natural setting and lovely views of the bay. When the fog rolls in, as it often does, the water turns a silvery-blue and the boats in the harbor are silhouetted against the rock formations and fir trees. Offshore is also **Prisoner's Rock,** where drunken sailors were once conducted by police to either sleep it off or immediately sober up by swimming back to town. A good place to take the children is the **Humboldt State University Marine Biology Laboratories** to see North Coast sea mammals and fish swimming in the aquarium.

*Motorcyclists put into perspective the size of **California's coastal redwoods.** The majestic redwoods can be appreciated while driving along the Redwood Highway (page 40). Right, the redwood forests contain creeks suitable for white-water canoeing.*

REDWOODS

California redwoods are the stateliest *living* monuments in the world. The trees once covered much of Greenland and Canada, but today are confined to the Sierra Nevada mountain range *(sequoia gigantea)* and the northern Pacific coast *(sequoia sempervirens).* The coastal species can reach a height of over 300 feet, and is long-lived; the oldest trees can reach an age of several hundred years. Apart from their beauty, redwoods are extremely hardy and resistant to fire and disease, and are thus a favorite target of the lumber industry. Entire California towns are constructed of redwood, and redwood furniture, decks, siding and refurnishings continue to be popular with consumers. Deforestation became a serious problem especially after World War II, and environmentalist lobby groups began to exert pressure on the federal government to protect the remaining stands of majestic redwoods.

Coastal redwoods are found as far south as Santa Cruz. The U.C. Santa Cruz campus is set in the hills above the town. College buildings are scattered among the redwood groves, and students also enjoy a spectacular vista of Monterey Bay. The redwoods in the immediate vicinity were felled for lumber until the establishment of the **Big Basin Redwoods State Park** and the **Henry Cowell Redwoods State Park.** Both parks offer a variety of scenic trails for the serious and non-serious hiker alike. A section of the Southern Pacific Railroad once connected the lumber camps with Santa Cruz, and a remnant of the line is now a favored excursion with visitors. A 100-year-old steam locomotive chugs from Felton to the Henry Cowell State Park amid towering redwood trees and Douglas firs.

Close to San Francisco, one historic reserve is the

*A **redwood log** is so wide that even a house can be made out of one.*

Muir Woods (page 27). Another is the Humboldt
Redwood State Park, located inland below
Ferndale and Eureka. At Humboldt, the old route to
Eureka, parallel to Highway 101, leads to a 30-mile
stretch known as Avenue of the Giants. Even taller
trees can be found in the park's Founder's Grove.
Wagon trains of pioneers would go through what is
now called the Shrine Drive-Thru-Tree, now a top
tourist attraction. The One-Log House also draws a
crowd. Camping is especially popular in the
Richardson Grove, as is kayaking in the Eel river,
which cuts across Humboldt Park.

The ecologists won a major victory in 1968 with the
creation of the Redwood National Park, a 40-mile
stretch north of Eureka between Orick and Crescent
City. The federally protected land comprises the
Prairie Creek Redwoods State Park (site of the
tallest trees in the world), the Del Norte Coast
Redwoods State Park and the Jedediah Smith State
Park. The spectacular redwoods, in the company of
Douglas firs and other evergreens, tower over the
ferns, wild flowers and a vast variety of flora,
including mushrooms. The redwoods thrive here
because of the high amount of rainfall, and the
moisture derived from coastal fog, prevalent
especially during the summer months. The
precipitation also gives rise to swift-moving creeks
and numerous larger waterways such as the
Redwood, Klamath and Smith rivers, teeming with
king salmon and steelhead trout. The hilly terrain
makes the spot a favorite with mountain bikers, and
the stone cliffs and rocky promontories represent a
challenge to the intrepid hiker. The Natural Park
Service, however, has tried to offer access to
everyone: Revelation Trail has tactile markers for
the blind, and a Braille guidebook is on sale at the
visitor's center.

The Redwood National Park was inaugurated by
Lady Bird Johnson among others, and the Lady Bird
Grove near the park entrance is named in honor of
a quasi-political figure who devoted much of her
time to beautifying America. The Tall Trees Grove

is the stuff of the Guinness World Book of Records; here is the tallest tree yet found, the **Howard Libby Redwood** (367 ft.). The sheer loveliness of nature here is best enjoyed on foot, yet an alternative exists in the form of a shuttle bus service (summer only). Visitors cluster on the **Douglas Memorial Bridge** to see the antics of harbor seals and sea lions. Roosevelt elk graze on the **Elk Prairie** as well as along the **Golden Bluffs,** which is also a perfect place for whale watching. The natural gorges, too, make for spectacular scenery, especially at **Fern Canyon,** where the walls are carpeted with fronds and moss. Don't miss a hike along the **Redwood Creek Trail** nor the **Coastal Trail.** And not just redwoods are preserved here: the **Prairie Creek Fish Hatchery** is set up specially for the propagation of trout.

There are many things to see in the **Klamath area,** which borders both the Prairie Creek and the Del Norte state parks. The **Klamath Overlook,** at the mouth of the Klamath River, is a fine place for whale watching. And, weddings are sometimes held under the impressive **Cathedral Tree,** actually a circular group of nine trees with a single root.

The only place where some tourist hype comes in is at the Del Norte park, which vaunts the **Trees of Mystery** in addition to giant redwood statues of the legendary lumberjack Paul Bunyan and his blue ox Babe.

The Jedediah Smith State Park was named after the first man who traveled overland from the Mississippi River to the Pacific Ocean. Smith passed through here in 1828, and came face to face with the awesome redwood groves. The **Stout Grove** contains trees characterized by 20-ft.-diameter trunks, and the trail of the same name leads to a sandy beach.

People often say that the mighty redwood trees impart a sense of deep spirituality. On the mundane side, however, the visitor can easily take home a souvenir of a trip to the Redwood National Park by stopping by the craft stands near the entrance. There, artisans carve redwood clocks, frames, knick-knacks and full-blown sculptures (even totem poles). No ecological code, however, has been violated: the wood comes from places not under the jurisdiction of the National Park Service.

Redwood lumber is used by artisans to fashion any number of useful objects.

REDWOOD HIGHWAY

Redwood trees line each side of the road along the
Redwood Highway, also known as U.S. Highway 101.
Nearly all the state's coastal redwood trees can be
found on the scenic route from Marin to Humboldt
counties, passing through groves in the Humboldt
Redwoods State Park and Grizzly Creek, up to the
far reaches of the Prairie Creek Redwoods State

Park, the Del Norte Coast Redwoods State Park and
the Jedediah Smith State Park, collectively known as
the Redwood National Park. The 300-mile excursion
through virgin wilderness makes for a pleasant
drive, especially if one's eventual destination is an
urban center. Sadly, some of the area is still a prime
target for the lumber industry, and trucks bearing
huge logs are not an infrequent sight on the
Redwood Highway (above). Business aside, the
Redwood Highway is an ideal place to stop and walk
in majestic surroundings.

Above, *the snow-capped peak of* **Mount Lassen.**

Below right, *completely frozen over in winter, the park's many* **lakes** *contain* **ice floes** *during the summertime.*

LASSEN VOLCANIC NATIONAL PARK

No one knows when Lassen Peak will blow its top again. The uncertainty, however, does not deter thousands of annual visitors to the **Lassen Volcanic National Park,** which extends over a vast radius of the southern Cascade mountain range. The volcanoes were originally mountains formed under the Pacific Ocean, and moved onto land by the shifting of the earth's plates. How a volcano is formed determines its composition and configuration, and thereby its type. Lassen Peak is a *plug dome volcano,* that is, a volcano engendered by rock pushing straight up a narrow shaft through a crater, with lava accumulating in a dome at the top. Geology aside, it is a four-to-five hour hike from the parking lot to the top of Lassen Peak (10,453 ft.), affording one the opportunity of a spectacular view of the rest of the park, and, on a clear day, Mount

Shasta and the Sacramento Valley. There are also a number of other trails for short and long hikes, and information on these, as well as on campsites, is supplied by the visitor's center.

One need not even get out of the car to observe most of the park's sights. Route 89, the main road, closed for most of the time from November to May because of deep snowdrifts, takes one up the steep embankments of Mount Lassen and down the other side. The scenery is dramatic: the colors are intense and the air so clear that it is noticeable. The higher the altitude, the more the pine forests recede, giving way to patches of yellow and brown volcanic rock. This bare landscape is made even more striking by the presence of fumaroles, holes in the earth from which hot gases and vapors rise.

Beautiful glacier lakes also abound, the most prominent being the shining **Emerald Lake, Manzanita Lake, Echo Lake, Lower Twin Lake, Butte Lake, Summit Lake, Juniper Lake** and **Lake Helen,** the latter named after Helen Tanner Brodt, the first woman to scale Mount Lassen in 1864. Many of these lakes are paradise for the fisherman, since they are stocked with rainbow trout. The turquoise

*Although **Lassen Peak** is dormant, volcanic activity abounds in the park.*

Right, *walkways provide access to the steam, mud and hot water of **Bumpass Hell**.*

blue water may look tempting on a hot day, but the temperatures are generally too cold for swimming. In fact, all year long snow caps Mount Lassen as well as other nearby peaks such as Brokeoff Mountain and Diamond Peak, and the lakes often contain ice floes, even in August. So summer visitors to the park in T-shirts and shorts can delight in scooping up wet snow with their hands on the lake shores. The one exception is **Boiling Springs Lake.** In this case, a trail passing through forests and meadows leads to a lake surrounded by muddy pools and jets of water and steam originating from cracks in the ground.

As could be expected, all four seasons are an impressive sight here. A profusion of wild flowers brightens the meadows during the summer. Nature is always buried under snow in the winter months, making the park a haven for sledders, cross-country and downhill skiers from November to April, weather permitting. Miles of paths around the park are open to the cross-country skier, who has the additional option of using the hiking trails and even the main road.

Lassen Peak last erupted between 1914 and 1915, and the effects of the event are visible in the **Devastated Area.** Molten rock, ash, cinders, smoke and extreme heat destroyed or damaged the wilderness, which is only now slowly coming back to life. As its name implies, the Lassen Volcanic National Park is also the site of intense thermal activity. A three-mile trail takes the sightseer through **Bumpass Hell,** a veritable cauldron of hot water, wells of bubbling mud and sulfurous smells. Remember to keep on the wooden walkway, though, as the discoverer of Bumpass Hell is reputed to have lost a leg here. More hot springs and steam are found at the **Sulphur Works;** ditto for the **Devil's Kitchen Trail** and **Little Hot Springs Valley.**

The national park was named after Peter Lassen, a Danish immigrant who founded a ranch in the Sacramento Valley.

MOUNT SHASTA

Shasta lends its name to a state historic park, caverns, a lake, a dam, a recreation area, a national forest, a town and a snow-capped volcano thought to be extinct. For a tour of all these places, start at **Mount Shasta** and slowly drive southward towards Redding.

The fifth tallest peak in California at 14,162 ft. (the tallest, Mount Whitney is 14,494 ft), Mount Shasta, like Lassen Peak, is part of the Cascade Range which extends through Oregon,Washington and British Columbia. Unlike Lassen Peak, Mount Shasta is a *composite* or *stratovolcano,* just like Japan's Mount Fuji, built upwards by the accumulation of volcanic ash, cinders and rock as well as lava flows.

Mount Shasta is visible for miles. Intense beauty is the order of the day, and there is an enormous sense of expanse and peacefulness. Every possible shade of green appears to be present in the predominantly evergreen forest, a sensation heightened by moss growing on tree bark. John Muir, who was to give his name to the Muir Woods, scaled Mount Shasta in

1874, and many people attempt the same feat every summer. The Shasta Indians revered a Great Spirit whom they believed resided within the peak, and today Mount Shasta is still a magnet for New Age followers certain that the mountain exudes a special type of energy.

Shasta City, a good jumping-off point for exploration of the region, is also home to a state-run **fish hatchery** specializing in baby trout.

The **Shasta National Forest** is on the way to the vast **Whiskeytown-Shasta-Trinity Recreational Area,** which comprises Whiskeytown Lake, Clair Engle Lake, the ski resorts of the Salmon-Trinity Alps, Shasta Dam, Lake Shasta and the Lake Shasta Caverns. All three lakes act as reservoirs for the Sacramento River and smaller rivers, and the water is used to irrigate the farmlands of the Central Valley. On a more relaxing note, boaters, water-skiers and windsurfers skim across the lakes' shining waters at high speed, and the surrounding man-made

beaches tend to be crowded in the summertime. Campers and hikers find the nearby woods a tranquil haven. **Shasta Lake** is populated with **houseboats,** floating trailers that can also be home as opposed to home away from home. For a unique experience, a houseboat can be rented, and after a few lessons, one is ready to leisurely explore the environs of Shasta Lake. A ferry takes passengers close to the **Shasta Caverns,** underground grottoes filled with crystal formations, small cascades, stalagmites and stalactites. The cavern's Cathedral Room is especially impressive due to the number of multicolor columns formed by the union of calcium carbonate on the floor (stalagmite) and calcareous water dripping from the cave roof (stalactite).

The final stop-off is the **Shasta State Historic Park,** near Redding. The site is an abandoned Gold Rush town complete with brick buildings, a jail and gallows. The former courthouse is now a museum chronicling the life of that period.

A floating community of houseboats on **Shasta Lake.**

*The arid countryside of the **Lava Beds** disguises the intricate natural passageways below ground.*

LAVA BEDS

North of Mount Shasta and close to the Oregon border is the **Lava Beds National Monument** which spreads out over 47,000 acres. Fierce volcanic activity over the centuries has produced a barren, desolate landscape characterized by black volcanic glass and volcanic ash cones of varying heights. The bleakness is enlivened only by the occasional presence of shrubs, pine trees, wild sage and juniper. The hot lava that once overwhelmed the area eventually cooled to leave behind a network of several hundred cylindrical underground tunnels and caverns, the main reason why people take the long drive to a national monument literally in the middle of nowhere.

The caves have an interesting history, having been used for defense by the local Modoc Indians against the U.S. Army in 1872. The U.S. government had earlier persuaded the Native Americans to move to a reservation in Oregon where they were treated badly by the Klamaths, another north Californian tribe who shared the same space. A group of Modocs decided to go home to the Lava Beds and, if necessary, fight it out under the guidance of their leader "Captain Jack." The solid rock of the Lava Beds acted as a natural fortress, and during the first skirmish 52 Modoc Indians defeated a troop of soldiers several times larger without a single casualty. They were to be defeated only four months later, and the survivors sent to a reservation in Oklahoma.

The now-peaceful scene of all this violence can be visited at **Captain Jack's Stronghold.** This fortification, and the other caves, can best be seen on a guided tour. Some sections of the Lava Beds National Monument bear a certain resemblance to the hiding places of the early Christians, hence the **Catacombs,** part of the 2-mile **Cave Loop Road** comprising the popular **Labyrinth** and the **Golden Dome.** The names of these underground chambers are fairly self-descriptive: some have incredibly high ceilings and others need to be crawled through to the other side.

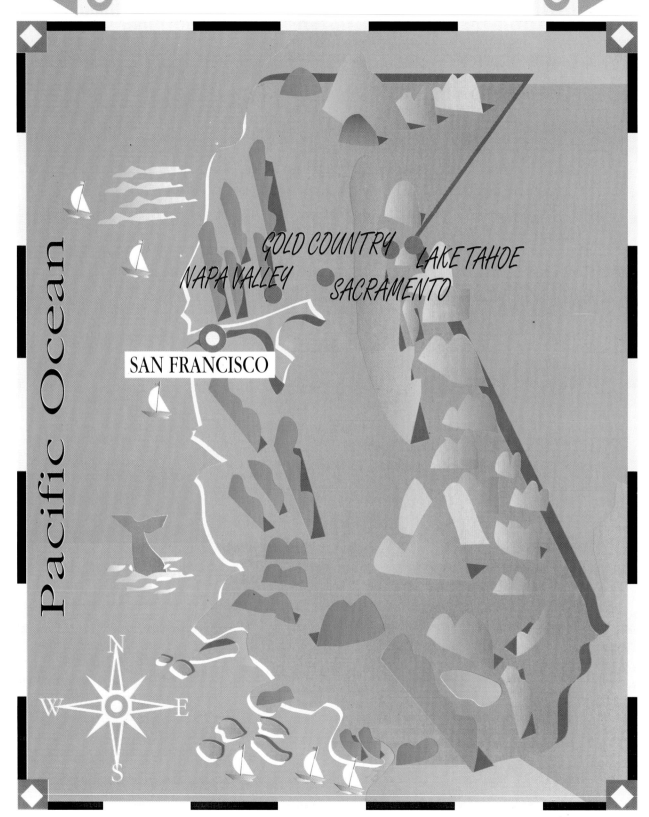

Pacific Ocean

GOLD COUNTRY

NAPA VALLEY

LAKE TAHOE

SACRAMENTO

SAN FRANCISCO

*The area has earned a reputation for **quality wines.***

THE WINE COUNTRY

The humble winepress is the unofficial symbol of the **Napa** and **Sonoma valleys,** places that catapulted California wines onto the international circuit. The Jesuit fathers cultivated the first vineyard in Sonoma during the 1820s in order to produce wine for Mass, but it wasn't until the 1970s that oenophiles sat up and noticed the area's quality Cabernet Sauvignon, Beaujolais, Merlot, Pinot Noir and Zinfandel (reds) as well as Pinot Chardonnay, Johannisberg Riesling, Sauvignon Blanc and Gewurztraminer (whites).

Since the Napa Valley's main highway tends to be crowded, keep in mind the pleasing alternatives of a **hot air balloon ride** or a ride on the **Wine Train** for a first impression of the Wine Country. A slow ascent in a hot air balloon is a gentle way of viewing a countryside composed of seemingly endless vineyards, rolling hills, small towns and cities. Back on the ground, the Wine Train takes the passengers from the city of Napa to St. Helena, where many of the Napa Valley's premier vineyards are concentrated. Tourists come here specially to tour the wineries and participate in a wine tasting. Stop-offs could include **Beringer, Mondavi, Beaulieu Vinyards, Sterling Vinyard** and **Charles Krug** (the entrance to the latter is pictured on page 55), all named after their original or present owners. The outstanding landmark at Beringer is the **Rhine House,** a Gothic wooden mansion constructed in 1883 by Frederick and Joseph Beringer and modeled on their home in Germany. The Beringers also built the estate's limestone caves for aging the wine in barrels. The Christian Brothers winery, too, was founded in the 1880s, before passing title to a Catholic educational order who knew (or evidently learned) how to make good wine. Charles Krug, on the other hand, first introduced wine making to the Napa Valley in 1861, and his legacy is carried on by the Peter Mondavi family.

The **Napa** and **Sonoma valleys** have soil and climatic conditions similar to that of Europe's great wine producing regions.

St. Helena is in the vicinity of Mount St. Helena, an extinct volcano which gave rise to the hot springs of **Calistoga,** the "Saratoga of California" envisaged by the resort's founder, and is located in the Napa Valley's northern perimeter. A relaxing way to spend (or end) a day in the area is to indulge in a mud bath, sauna or massage here.

The Napa Valley has even been the source of literary inspiration: an abandoned bunkhouse near a silver mine provided a home for honeymooners Robert Louis Stevenson and Fanny Osborne. Stevenson had met his future wife, then married to someone else, in Europe, and followed her back to the United States. He immortalized Mount St. Helena as Spyglass Hill in *Treasure Island,* and the vicinity where the couple lived for a time has been turned into the **Robert Louis Stevenson State Park.**

Always on a literary note, **Sonoma County** was the home of author Jack London (1876-1916) who poetically dubbed it "the Valley of the Moon." He built the "Wolf House" (destroyed by arson) near Glen Ellen, and a museum has been set up on the property, now the **Jack London State Park.**

Hot air ballooning is one way to see the Napa Valley; both Napa and Sonoma vineyards allow visitors to visit the **wine cellars** and observe the various phases of wine making.

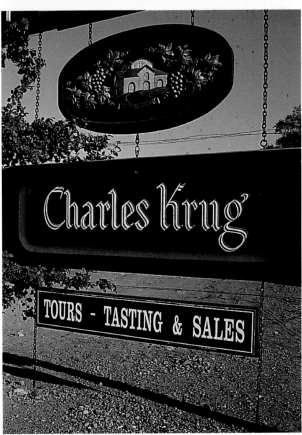

Before taking off to the county wineries and those in the adjacent Russian River Valley, the town of Sonoma merits a visit. Buildings of an historical interest are clustered in and around the **Sonoma Plaza.** Modern-day Sonoma had its roots in the **Mission San Francisco Solano,** founded in the 1820s by Spanish fathers as the very last of 21 Catholic outposts in California, which, by then, was part of Mexico. The mission was made of adobe, as were the army barracks and the home of General Vallejo, the Mexican commander.

The old part of town was also the setting of the famous Bear Flag Revolt. In 1846 Mexico decided to expel all Americans from California, which incited John C. Fremont and a band of 30 rebels to take possession of Sonoma under the Bear Flag. The victors proclaimed an independent "California Republic" on June 14, 1846, (the date later became Flag Day) which lasted until July 7th when the U.S. annexed the entire territory without firing a shot.

The **State Capitol** is the building most closely identified with **Sacramento**.

SACRAMENTO

 Location, gold and transportation are what turned **Sacramento** into a thriving city and the capital of California. Sacramento is located north of San Francisco at the junction of the Sacramento and American rivers in the fertile Sacramento Valley. An enormous area, stretching all the way to the Sierra Nevada foothills, was initially given to Swiss immigrant John Sutter as a land grant by the Mexican government. Sutter arrived at the present site of Sacramento in 1839 to establish a community based on agriculture, livestock and trade which he called "New Helvetia," even going so far as to buy all the furnishings of Fort Ross, a Russian settlement on the coast. Ironically, he was ruined by the discovery of gold on the eastern part of his property in 1848: Sutter's workers deserted him and his land was overrun by thousands of prospectors. His son was instrumental in founding

the city of Sacramento the following year, but Sutter was to die a broken man in 1880.

Sacramento, on the other hand, thrived as the point of entry to the Gold Country; a railway connecting the fledgling city with Folsom was inaugurated in 1856, and the western junction of the Pony Express opened for business here in 1860. Due to its strategic importance, Sacramento was proclaimed the state capital in 1864. Thus, the **State Capitol Building** (pictured above and to the right) is the image most closely identified with the city. This domed neoclassical building has been restored to its late-19th century splendor, and is open to visitors, as is the surrounding **Capitol Park.** The former boasts marble mosaic floors, oak staircases, gilt and crystal; the latter has one of the most extensive collections of plants and trees in the country. Not far away is the **Old Governor's Mansion,** a white Victorian house completed in the 1870s and the sumptuous home of

California governors up to Ronald Reagan. East of the government complex is **Sutter's Fort,** a reconstruction of the pioneer settlement complete with a few original adobe walls and several artisan workshops. By Sutter's time, most of the Native Americans in the area had died of disease due to sporadic contact with white men, but their presence is remembered in the nearby **Indian Museum**.

Sacramento grew around the waterfront, and some of the steamboats and paddle wheelers which used to ply the river between the city and San Francisco are still docked here, used, as in the case of the **Delta King,** as floating hotels or for short/long cruises (page 58). The city's past has also been preserved here, in **Old Sacramento,** and a good introduction to that period is given in the **Sacramento History Museum,** which proudly houses the gold nuggets that spurred the onslaught of fortune seekers.

How transportation was vital to the area's history and development is nowhere more evident than in Old Sacramento. The first stop-off on a theme-related walking tour could be at the **Huntington, Hawkins & Co. Store,** a one-time hardware store where the so-called "Big Four" — Charles Crocker, Mark Hopkins, Collis P. Huntington and Leland Stanford — decided to start the Central Pacific Railroad Company, a decision that was to contribute to the city's growth. Spurred on by Theodore Judah, the engineer who designed the Sacramento-Folsom track, and by government subsidies, the "Big Four" managed to realize their dream of connecting Sacramento to the East Coast via railway. With a lot of Chinese-American labor involved at the western end, the Central Pacific and the Union Pacific railroads joined in Promontory, Utah on May 10, 1869 to form a transcontinental rail link. Several decades of railroad history are preserved in the elegant, turn-of-the-century locomotives and sleeping cars of the **California State Railroad Museum,** all perfectly restored, much to the onlooker's delight. The same museum ticket allows the visitor to enter the

*A close-up of a sculpture on the **State Capitol facade** depicting a grizzly bear attacking a Native American during California's pioneer days.*

stupendous **Central Pacific Railroad Station**, while there is an extra charge to take a ride on a steam-powered train during the summer months. The 1853 Wells Fargo building, presently known as the **B.F. Hastings Building,** is home to the one-time Pony Express headquarters (now a museum) and is the original chambers of the California Supreme Court, dating back to 1854.

Transportation has become so associated with Old Sacramento that it even contains the **Towe Ford Museum,** a collection of vintage automobiles from 1903 to the 1960s. Aficionados and non will enjoy seeing the evolution of the Ford car and comparing styles, since each year is represented with a corresponding model.

Cultural attractions of Old Sacramento include the **Eagle Theater** and the **Crocker Art Museum.** Drama is still performed at the Eagle Theater, a faithful reconstruction of the 1849 edifice, while the Crocker Art Museum, based on the collections of E.B. Crocker, brother of Charles, the railroad baron, is situated in an authentic 19th century building. There is an overview of European, American and Asian art.

Above: a **paddle wheeler** brings to mind the fact that Sacramento's fortune has been favored by its location at the junction of the American and Sacramento rivers.

Below and right: **Old Sacramento** provides an interesting glimpse into the city's history.

GOLD COUNTRY

"There's GOLD in them thar hills." It took exactly a year from John Marshall's discovery on January 28, 1848 for word to get out, and then the '49ers descended en masse on the Sierra Nevada foothills. The prospectors were searching for a quick fortune in "placer gold," i.e. loose gold found in rivers and dirt, much as Marshall did when he found a gold nugget in a canal leading to John Sutter's sawmill. The boom lasted for much of the 1850s, and when the readily available "color" (as gold came to be known) was exhausted, the ingenious method of hydraulic mining, involving the blasting away of hillsides with a jet of pressurized water, was devised. From the 1860s onwards, costly conventional gold mining methods became the rule, and most of the Gold Country went bust, leaving behind windswept landscapes, ghost towns and a cast of characters that would become part of the American legend.

The **Marshall Gold Discovery State Historic Park**

*A favorite destination of visitors, the **Mother Lode country** represents a colorful and perfectly preserved part of California's past.*

near **Coloma** is a good place to initiate a foray into gold country. Sutter's sawmill and Marshall's cabin have been carefully reconstructed according to the original designs, and a museum provides insight into the events which took place here.

The Gold Country is divided into the Northern and Southern mine areas with Coloma roughly in the middle. To the north, the **Old Town** in **Auburn** is very much worth a visit. **Nevada City** has some fine Victorian homes, as well as the unusual **Malakoff Diggings,** a man-made gorge distinguished by colored pinnacles, the result of overzealous hydraulic mining.

To the south, Philip Armour sold meat and John Studebaker wheelbarrows, thereby making their fortunes, in **Placerville,** once known as "Hangtown." **Drytown** is the ironic name of a locality that once boasted 27 active saloons. Samuel Clemens (Mark Twain) first heard the tale which inspired *The Jumping Frog of Calaveras County* in **Angels Camp,** and both **Columbia** and **Coulterville,** once settings for *High Noon,* are state historic landmarks.

*Nearly every kind of winter and summer sport can be practiced on and around **Lake Tahoe,** one of California's most verdant areas. Above, the **Emerald Bay** received its name from the color of its sparkling waters.*

LAKE TAHOE

Little did John C. Fremont and Kit Carson dream when they sighted Lake Tahoe in 1844 that the area would become California's playground. At that time the forests were inhabited by the Washoe Indians, for whom hunting and fishing were means of survival as opposed to their use in today's recreation. After Fremont and Carson, pioneers, on their way to California or the silver mines of Nevada's Comstock Lode, would pass close to Lake Tahoe without stopping. It wasn't until the 1920s and

'30s that vacation homes began to be built on the lakeshore, and after World War II people started to spend their weekends in the wilderness here.

For Lake Tahoe offers wonderful downhill and cross-country skiing in the winter, as well as backpacking, camping, waterskiing, boating, fishing, sunbathing, swimming (for hardy souls not afraid of cold water), biking and golfing during the warm weather. Of course, there is live entertainment and gambling on the Nevada side all year round.

Despite man's incursion, the sapphire-colored lake and its environs have remained relatively unspoiled. Lake Tahoe's statistics alone are impressive: it is 22

miles long, 12 miles across and its depth is over 1500 ft. in spots, so deep that the waters never freeze. Nestled in the granite peaks of the Sierra Nevada mountains 6,000 ft. above sea level, two-thirds of Lake Tahoe lies within the boundaries of California, and one-third in Nevada. The lake is surrounded by land which is for the most part protected by federal law: **Tahoe National Forest, Desolation Wilderness, Eldorado National Forest** and the **Toiyabe National Forest.** The major towns are South Lake Tahoe and Tahoe City. **Squaw Valley,** the site of the 1960 Winter Olympics, is in the vicinity of Tahoe City, while the **Heavenly Valley Ski Resort** close to South Lake Tahoe is also

popular. At the latter, non-skiers enjoy taking the tram to the top of the mountain, a breathtaking 8,200 feet above sea level. Also on the lake's southern side is the breathtaking **Emerald Bay State Park,** situated around a natural inlet, and a good view of the bay can be had from **Eagle Falls.** An adventuresome soul built a replica of a medieval Scandinavian residence within the park during the 1920s and the so-called **Vikingsholm** continues to be popular with tourists even today. Back to nature, the ponderosa pine is widespread in the forest, lending its name to the ranch of the popular T.V. series *Bonanza*, which can be visited over the California border near Incline Village, Nevada.

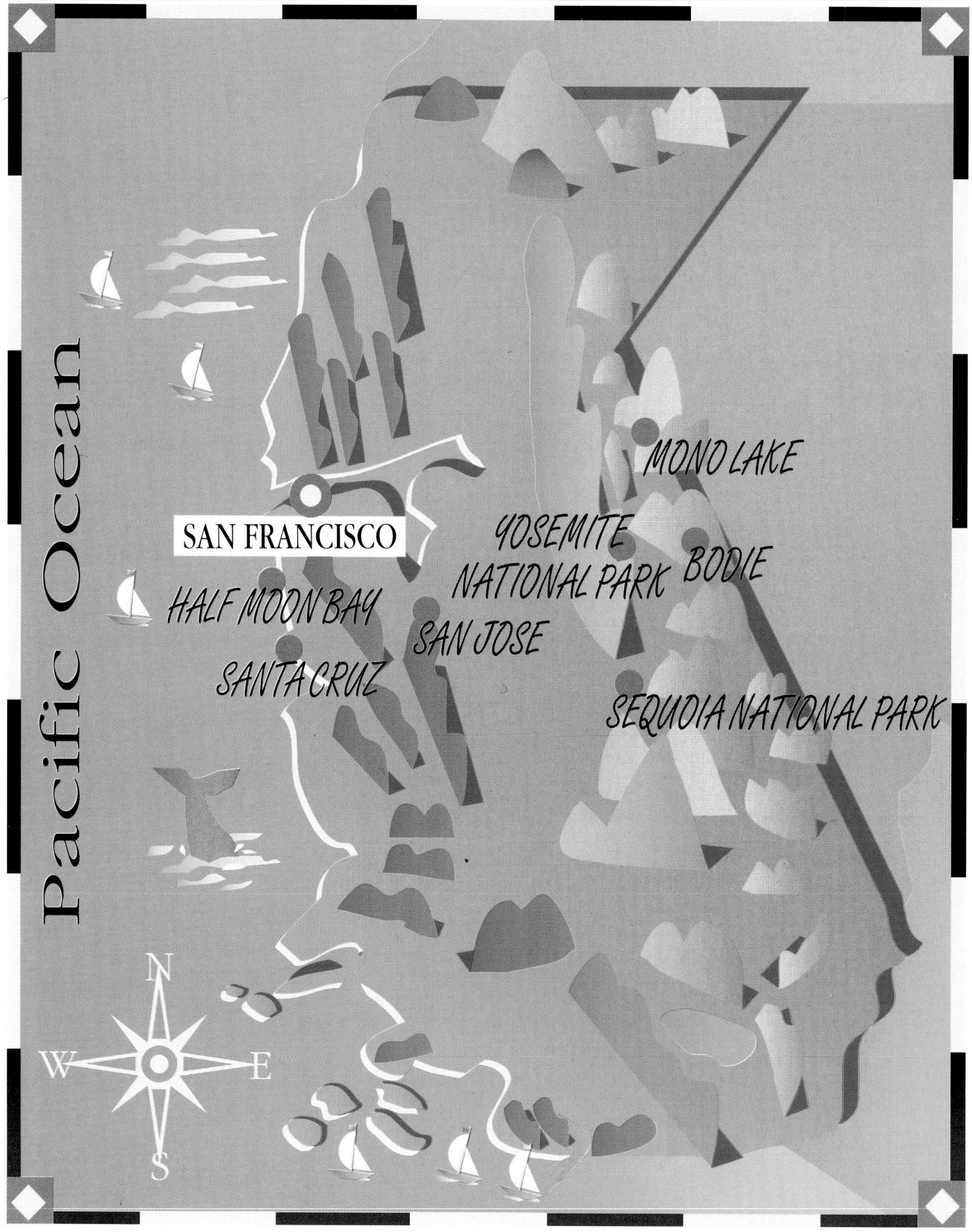

Pacific Ocean

MONO LAKE

SAN FRANCISCO

YOSEMITE
NATIONAL PARK BODIE

HALF MOON BAY

SAN JOSE

SANTA CRUZ

SEQUOIA NATIONAL PARK

N
W E
S

*The beautiful proportions of **El Capitan's smooth granite face** (above, left) makes it appear much smaller than its actual size.*

YOSEMITE NATIONAL PARK

Yosemite, one of nature's finest masterpieces, is located near the geographical center of the Great Sierra Nevada Mountain Range. The majesty and grandeur of the massive granite walls, the power of the spectacular waterfalls and the serene beauty of the valley floor combine to create magnificent vistas in every direction. Yosemite Valley and its surroundings were formed over hundreds of thousands of years as a result of uplifting in the earth's crust, the activity of glaciers and erosion. Ancient ice scars can still be seen today on the giant granite domes created by glaciers and later by the Merced River. The Miwok tribe lived in the area until the advent of the white man in the second half of the nineteenth century. In 1864, Abraham Lincoln signed an Act of Congress granting Yosemite to the state of California to be preserved intact for future generations. Theodore Roosevelt visited Yosemite in 1903, and three years later he signed a bill placing Yosemite Valley and the Mariposa Grove under the jurisdiction of the federal government. Over 3,000,000 people visit the park each year.

Yosemite's natural cascades are **Ribbon Fall, Bridalveil Fall, Yosemite Falls, Vernal Fall** and **Nevada Fall.** A mesmerizing sight for early season travelers who catch the falls in full force, many late summer and autumn visitors are disappointed when they come face-to-face with dry, barren rock. Yosemite's waterfalls are dependent on the winter snow: a rapid melt or a low water content determines just how long the water flows.

RIBBON FALL

BRIDALVEIL FALL

EL CAPITAN

THREE BROTHERS

CATHEDRAL ROCKS

YOSEMITE FALLS

SENTINEL ROC

YOSEMITE VILLAGE

ROYAL ARCHES

GLACIER POINT

MIRROR LAKE

HALF DOME

VERNAL FALL

NEVADA FALL

Bevins '93

Yosemite Valley as seen from Tunnel view turnout.

Sometimes prolonged by heavy summer thunderstorms, the falls capacity can visibly swell to torrential proportions.

The first two can be easily viewed from the valley floor. **Ribbon Fall** is the longest waterfall in the valley at 1,612 ft., but usually dries up during July and August. The **Bridalveil Fall** drops down 620 ft. all year round although the flow is slight in the late summer. Quite possibly the most spectacular display of water in the valley is **Yosemite Falls,** which is over 2,400 ft. in height, and can be reached by a strenuous climb. One of the most beautiful and popular hiking trails leads to the **Vernal** and **Nevada Falls.** Aptly named the Mist Trail, the path is so close to the thundering waters that rock climbers are often drenched in mist. The reward comes with a rest by the Emerald Pool at the top of Vernal Fall before continuing to the equally beautiful scenery of Nevada Fall, which leaps from a narrow spout and tumbles down 594 ft. The view of both can also be enjoyed from a distance by driving to Glacier Point.

One of Yosemite's most famous landmarks is **El Capitan,** smooth granite that rises into a single dramatic rock wall. The steep rounded peak ascends 3,000 ft. towards the sky, a mecca for climbers from around the world. El Capitan is the guardian of the entrance to Yosemite Valley.

Yosemite is also known for its rock formations. Best visible from El Capitan bridge and meadow are the **Cathedral Rocks,** averaging 2,000 ft. in height from the valley floor. Also known as the Three Graces, the Cathedral Rocks were christened in 1862 by James Hutchings, an early park resident. The **Three Brothers,** on the other hand, were named in honor of Chief Tenaya's three sons. Converging upwards like the gables of a church, these blocks of granite owe their form to fractures in the rock that geologically crisscross the Sierras. The highest point, **Eagle Peak,** is 7,779 ft. The same triangulation of the cliffs is apparent in Glacier Point and to the right of Indian Canyon. **Sentinel Rock,** above the valley floor, one of the more dramatic granite outcroppings that loom over the valley, was formed by glacial action during the Ice Age. **Sentinel Fall** can be seen to the right of the rock, behind which is **Sentinel Dome** (8,122 ft), accessible only by foot.

The view from **Glacier Point** gives the visitor a chance to get a clear perspective of the layout of

Yosemite National Park. Directly below, overlooking a sheer 3,000 ft. drop is the Curry Village complex. Even more amazing is the sweep of mountains bordering the parkland. Breathtaking panoramas of the High Sierra encircle the visitor. On a clear day, summits can be seen that rise at least 50 miles from Glacier Point. In between is a vast wonderland of carved granite that looks like frozen waves on a storm-tossed sea. Glaciers once blanketed this granite wilderness, creating the wonderful shapes that can be admired today.

Half Dome rises majestically 4,882 ft. above the valley floor at its eastern end. During the summer and early fall months, the summit can be reached by following an eight-and-a-half mile trail which starts at the Happy Isles. The first successful climb of Half Dome was achieved by George Anderson in October 1875. Not many people, however, went to the top until the Sierra Club erected the first set of steel cables in 1919. Lichens and algae grow on the slippery surface.

Possibly the most spectacular display of water in the park are **Bridalveil Fall** *(bottom) and* **Yosemite Falls** *(right). The flow depends on winter snowfalls and summer thunderstorms.*

Following pages, glacier action created the **Liberty Cap** *(left) and the sheer, 2,000-ft.-steep face of the* **Half Dome** *monolith.*

MONO LAKE

The town of Lee Vining happens to be the eastern gateway to Yosemite National Park and the western gateway to another natural marvel, **Mono Lake**. With all the shifting of the earth's plates during the various geological eras, Mono Lake is what is left of the sea trapped inland some 700,000 to a million years ago, and Mark Twain rightly called it "the Dead Sea of the West." Mono Lake is both extremely salty (three times more than the ocean) and highly alkaline, characteristics steadily on the increase since 1941, the year the Los Angeles Department of Water and Power started tapping it for drinking water. As early as the turn of the century, Los Angeles city fathers began worrying about a

water shortage, and just before World War I, commissioned an aqueduct in the Owen Valley not far from Mono Lake. The plentiful waters of the Sierra Nevada mountain range were thus effectively deviated southward, but L.A.'s thirst turned out to be unquenchable, and a tunnel was constructed connecting Mono Lake to the aqueduct in 1941. The unfortunate result is that Mono Lake has shrunk to its present size — it is eight miles long and 13 miles wide — and the natural ecosystem has suffered greatly as well.

Although Mono Lake has no outlets, a number of streams feed into it and springs bubble up from beneath the lake bed. The impact of the calcium in the fresh water and the carbonate in the lake's salt water has created limestone stalagmites which in turn have slowly come to the surface during the drainage process. The water level has dropped nearly 50 ft. since the '40s, and the chalky tufa spires are now the landscape's distinguishing feature. The pinnacles are beautifully reflected in Mono Lake's gray-blue waters along with the majestic Sierra Nevada snow-capped mountain peaks.

There are no fish in the lake, which is home to algae, brine flies, salt water shrimp and crabs, a diet perfect for sea gulls and other migrant water fowl. "Mono" is the Yokut tribal word for fly, and one can assume that California sea gulls have feasted on these insects for thousands of years. The birds have traditionally nested on the islands of Paoha and Negit. Their habitats, however, are threatened because peninsulas linking the islands to the shore have been formed as the water recedes, thus allowing access to natural enemies such as the coyote. Environmentalists have been up in arms for years, to little avail.

The **Mono Basin National Forest Scenic Area** encompassing the lake and the surrounding land was declared as such by Congress in 1984, and can be toured on foot, by car, canoe and even via cross-country skis. Many of the distinctive calcium carbonate formations are located in **South Tufa Grove,** not far from **Navy Beach.** Due to the lake's high saline content, it is virtually impossible to sink while swimming! The Scenic Area also includes miles of salt flats, extinct volcanoes and volcanic craters; one example of the latter is the **Panum Crater.**

*The tufa towers of **Mono Lake** have emerged since World War II because Los Angeles has been steadily draining the area of its vital natural water supply.*

*Legend holds that a shooting took place every day in the gold mining town of **Bodie**. Artifacts from the past are in a remarkable state of preservation, from vintage cars and buggies (left) to the buildings themselves (above).*

BODIE

Bodie is the quintessential California Gold Rush ghost town populated by dust, tumbleweeds and the occasional tourist. Remarkably preserved because of its isolated position in the high desert, Bodie had a reputation as a fast-living and fast-dying town from the early 1850s until it was definitively abandoned in the early 1900s. Bodie's wealth did not come from "placer gold," that is, gold panned in creeks, but from nearby mines that yielded millions of dollars in assets. The citizens of Bodie, 10,000 strong, won recognition as an especially lawless bunch, giving rise to a legend that a murder was committed in the town before sunup every day. Its saloons were reputedly proud of having on hand the worst whiskey of all the mining camps. Bodie's fancy ladies were especially famous; even the notorious "Madame Moustache" decided to make her final home and eternal resting place here. "Madame Moustache"

came into the world as Eleanor Dumont, and, as a young woman with a captivating French accent, operated a highly successful gambling house in Nevada City. Mining camps and miners were both her passion and downfall: she ended up as the hardened "Madame Moustache" who committed suicide in 1879.

There are about 150 wooden buildings left in Bodie, only a small percentage of the original settlement. What remains — the homes, the church and the funeral parlor — is conserved as the **Bodie State Historic Park.** The state of California does only a minimum of upkeep, thus contributing to the sense of decline that is entirely in tune with the setting. The inhabitants apparently came away in a great hurry, for many of their belongings were left behind, from curtains, furniture and oil paintings to personal effects such as clothing. Some of these are kept in a small museum located in the **Miner's Union Building.** Bodie is best visited in spring and summer since the road leading to it north of Lee Vining is generally covered with snow during the winter months.

SEQUOIA AND KINGS CANYON NATIONAL PARKS

Unjustly overlooked by many visitors are the Sequoia and Kings Canyon National Parks, neighboring enclaves of the *sequoia gigantea,* the Sierra Nevada sequoia tree. In contrast to its tall and slender cousin the coastal redwood *(sequoia sempervirens)*, the sequoia has two outstanding characteristics: an exceptional longevity and an extremely wide trunk. Coastal redwoods generally attain an age of "only" several hundred years, while several-thousand-year-old sequoias are not uncommon.

The most spectacular sequoias are, naturally, in the Sequoia National Park's **Giant Forest,** home to the General Sherman Tree, immortalized in the Guinness World Book of Records thanks to its height (275 ft.) and width (36 ft.). Take the Congress Trail for a walking tour of the grove and admire other mighty sequoias such as the President Lincoln and the President McKinley trees. Confirming the fairytale-like setting is the abundance of fairytale-like place names. One is the **Crystal Cave,** nestled deep in solid rock, and overlaid with stalagmites and stalactites. The **Lost Grove** is where a number of trees with 15-to-20 ft. trunks are found, and the best view can be had from the granite **Moro Rock.** Finally, the High Sierra Trail joins up with the John Muir Trail to lead to **Mount Whitney**, at 14,491 ft. the highest North American peak outside Alaska.

The Kings Canyon Park is not without its interesting sights. Sheer canyon walls drop down to the **Kings River,** originally *Rio de los Santos Reyes,* named by a Spanish expedition in 1805 in honor of the Three Kings in the New Testament. The 267-ft. Grant Tree, along with the Robert E. Lee Tree, is located in **Grant Grove,** and the **Big Stump Area** is a vivid example of what environmentalists have fought so hard to avoid.

*The **Sierra Nevada sequoia tree** is shorter than its cousin, the coastal redwood, and has a wider trunk.*

*Many of **California's pumpkins** come from **Half Moon Bay**, and Halloween is celebrated here like nowhere else.*

HALF MOON BAY

Back to the Pacific ocean, the charming village of **Half Moon Bay** derives its name from the nearby crescent-shaped bay. It is probable that Sir Francis Drake, the first European to set foot in northern California, actually saw Half Moon Bay during his voyage up the coast in 1579. At a certain point Drake did land on the coast to claim "Nova Albion" for Queen Elizabeth I and her descendants. What has remained obscure down to the present day is actual location of this famous event. The theories range from Bolinas and Bodega bays in the north, to San Francisco Bay, and even Santa Barbara. Popular credence, however, holds that the English adventurer's ship dropped anchor along the Point Reyes peninsula where Drake's Bay is found.

In 1769, Gaspar de Portola led an expedition northward from San Diego on the lookout for Monterey Bay, which had been glowingly described by Sebastian Vizcaino more than a century earlier. An expedition of Portola's men stood on what is now Sweeney's ridge in Half Moon Bay and discovered San Francisco Bay and the Golden Gate.

The town of Half Moon Bay was settled in the mid-nineteenth century by Italian, Portuguese and Chilean immigrants, and their descendants continue to celebrate a **Pentecost Festival** every spring. The town's economy has always been based on income derived from fishing and agriculture, the latter centered initially around artichokes and Brussel sprouts and later on... pumpkins! As could be expected, the month of October is an especially festive time to visit, and the special events include an **Art and Pumpkin Festival,** culminating in Half Moon Bay's famous pumpkin parade. During the festival, the village is a haven for scarecrows, jack o' lanterns and costumed trick-or-treaters, and the New England atmosphere is further heightened by the presence of vintage Victorian homes. The village has many delightful shops and restaurants in addition to miles of sandy beach and a busy harbor.

SAN JOSE AND SANTA CRUZ

San Jose could easily be the dream-come-true of a corporate marketing department. Thanks to its strategic location smack in the center of California, the one-time placid farming town in the Santa Clara Valley has turned into the bustling high-tech capital of the Silicon Valley, headquarters for firms connected with the computer, chemical or aerospace industry. San Jose is one of California's oldest and fastest-growing towns, and for a brief time was even the state capital before Sacramento. The visitor who comes here not for business reasons will probably want to see the **Winchester Mystery House** and the **Rosicrucian Museum.** Sarah Winchester, an extremely superstitious woman, assuaged her guilt about inheriting the Winchester rifle fortune by personally designing a massive Victorian mansion with staircases that end abruptly and doors that open onto walls. The Rosicrucian Museum houses Assyrian, Babylonian and Egyptian collections.

Life in Santa Cruz, however, is as laid back as it is frenetic in San Jose. Facing the Monterey Bay south of San Jose, Santa Cruz was founded as a port from which to ship redwood lumber in the 19th century, and later became a resort and college town. A melange of influences create a unique atmosphere in Santa Cruz. The Spanish founded **Mission Santa Cruz** (Holy Cross) in 1794, and a reconstruction of the original, destroyed in an earthquake, faithfully mirrors the mission spirit. Surrounding farms produce a bumper crop of brussel sprouts and artichokes, while the actual town is a magnet for casually-dressed tourists who stroll along the sandy shore and the **Santa Cruz Beach Boardwalk.** A throwback to an earlier era, the boardwalk offers such delights as a penny arcade, a lovely 1911 merry-go-round known as **Looff Carousel,** and the **Giant Dipper,** a 1924 roller coaster. U.C. Santa Cruz students have brought their own brand of political and environment activism to the town, along with alternative lifestyles.

Above, *San Jose* has enjoyed the benefits of a business boom and a consequent population explosion in recent years.

Below, a view of *Santa Cruz,* known for its beaches as well as artistic and intellectual activity.

Pacific Ocean

SAN FRANCISCO

MONTEREY
CANNERY ROW
POINT LOBOS
BIG SUR
HEARST CASTLE
MORRO BAY
SOLVANG
SANTA BARBARA
VENTURA
OXNARD
LOS ANGELES

N
W E
S

*A birds-eye view of the **Monterey harbor.** Fishing was once the primary means of livelihood here; now it is tourism.*

MONTEREY

Much as it was when Sebastian Vizcaino first described it, the shoreline of Monterey Peninsula is a nature poem of azure sea, shimmering fish, white beaches, rocky cliffs, cypress trees, raucous birds and capricious sea animals. In 1602 the Spanish explorer sailed into the bay, and upon landing, named the area after the Count of Monte Rey, a viceroy of New Spain, and sailed out again. Bounded to the north by Monterey Bay, and to the west by Carmel Bay, the Monterey Peninsula has retained large stretches of unspoiled territory over the 17-Mile Drive, the Del Monte Forest, down through the Point Lobos State Reserve and Big Sur. Farmland, vineyards which make notably fine wines and small communities, each with its own special character, are interspersed throughout the remaining area.

Echoes of the Spanish past are found on the Monterey Path of History, while the unique sea life and habitats of Monterey Bay are on view in the city's Aquarium. Ironically, the latter is located in a former sardine processing plant on Cannery Row. The Point Pinos Lighthouse is the West Coast's oldest continuously working beacon. Even its style is interesting, reminiscent as it is of New England architecture, a fitting prelude to the Victorian clapboard houses of Pacific Grove. The name Pebble Beach immediately conjures images of well-groomed golf courses, prestigious golf tournaments and big prize money. Artists, writers and movie stars dwell in tiny Carmel, where the locals have taken great pains to maintain it as a small village, although some of the boutiques and art galleries are worthy of a big city. Father Junipero Serra's spirit (as well as his body) is serenely preserved within the dreamlike Moorish architecture of the Carmel Mission, also known as the Mission San Carlos Borromeo. Further inland, only a short distance from the Monterey Peninsula shoreline where it all began, fruit and vegetables are grown in the Salinas Valley — John Steinbeck country.

Left, the *"Lone Cypress"* on the 17-Mile-Drive is the instantly-recognized emblem of the Monterey Peninsula. The species is found only in this part of California. (Reproduced with permission of the Pebble Beach Corporation).

The catch of the day is still sold in the old-time marine ambiance, complete with sea lions, of **Old Fisherman's Wharf,** Monterey.

The two landmarks most closely identified with the Monterey Peninsula are the **Old Fisherman's Wharf** and the **17-Mile Drive**.

In the 1850s, Portuguese and American sailors discovered a good source of income in whaling. These hardy souls were subsequently supplanted by an international group of fisherman in search of smaller prey. This next generation of seafaring men would sail out in the dark of the night and return during daylight hours, boats brimming with shrimp, salmon, albacore, squid, mackerel and rock cod. The crews were composed of immigrant Italians, Chinese, Japanese and a number of local residents. At the beginning of the 20th century, attention increasingly turned to Monterey Bay sardines. Small as these fish are, sardines meant big business to both Fisherman's Wharf, where they were hauled in, and the adjacent Cannery Row, where they were processed. Then, in 1950, the very last Monterey Bay sardine was canned, and Fisherman's Wharf began yet a new phase of its existence, that of a tourist attraction.

The 17-Mile Drive is a twisting, turning road which encompasses much of the natural and man-made beauty of the southwestern Monterey Peninsula. It begins in Pacific Grove, continues parallel to the Monterey Bay Country Club, then swings along the Pacific Ocean coastline down to Pebble Beach and Carmel Bay. The Drive is famous for its breath-taking panorama: cliffs of sheer rock, seals, sandpipers, cypress trees gnarled by the wind, waves breaking into white foam and bracing salt spray. The trees, known as the "Monterey cypress," belong to a species peculiar to the Monterey Peninsula that thrive on the harsh conditions by the sea. Robert Louis Stevenson called them "ghosts fleeing before the wind." Emblematic of both the 17-Mile Drive and the Monterey Peninsula is the much-photographed and much-loved **"Lone Cypress"** (left), close to Midway Point. The oldest trees, some close to 500 years old, are found in the Crocker Grove.

*Above, not far offshore from Monterey is a chasm so deep that it could contain the Grand Canyon twice over, allowing whales, dolphins, porpoises and other marine life to swim much closer to the harbor than would be normally possible. The native sea mammals, fish and birds can be viewed close up at the **Monterey Bay Aquarium** (left).*

Looking straight towards the horizon, one can appreciate the scenic beauty of **Monterey Bay,** due in large part to its unique geological formation. Not far offshore is a chasm so deep that it could contain the Grand Canyon twice over, and this allows whales, dolphins and porpoises to swim closer to the harbor than would be normally expected. During the summer, a phenomenon called "upwelling" occurs: nutrient-rich waters from the depth of this sea canyon come to the surface and then flow into shallower waters around the coast, thus providing food for many species of marine life. Sea lions, gulls, terns and pelicans also receive food from human hands at Fisherman's Wharf. The waterfront is heavily populated by small harbor seals, large elephant seals and amusing sea otters, the mascots of Monterey Bay. Once hunted almost to extinction for its thick fur, the protected sea otter now spends most of its time floating on its back, often cradling either its offspring or dinner on its stomach. The animals eat up to 25% of their weight in food each day.

The **Monterey Bay Aquarium** is the dream come true of four local marine biologists who wished to share their vision with the general public. In 1980, they formed the nucleus of a foundation whose aim was to adapt the abandoned Hovden Cannery on Cannery Row into a home for the plants, fish, birds and marine mammals native to Monterey Bay. How well the group succeeded can be measured by the overwhelming number of visitors who tour the Aquarium exhibits every year. They come to see live sardines, mackerel and other fish weave in and out of the *Kelp Forest,* and the sandy sea floor, deep granite reefs, shale reefs, and encrusted wharf pilings of the *Monterey Bay Habitats.* Here, sharks cut an arc across waters shared with king salmon and striped bass; lower down, sand dabs and hermit crabs move smoothly on the sand. Close to the surface, dark mussels tenaciously cling to the dock in the company of colorful barnacles.

Above, *Monterey's **Cannery Row** entered the nation's consciousness thanks to the John Steinbeck novel of the same name. Today, the original sardine processing plants are now sites for restaurants, shops and boutiques. Top right, the **Perry House** displays a combination of Spanish and New England architectural elements which distinguishes the "Monterey style."* Bottom right, *the **Royal Presidio Chapel** was constructed by the first Spanish settlers in 1794.*

CANNERY ROW AND OLD MONTEREY

As John Steinbeck wrote, **"Cannery Row** in Monterey in California is a poem, a stink, a grating noise, a quality of light, a tone, a habit, a nostalgia, a dream. Cannery Row is the gathered and scattered, tin and iron and rust and splintered wood, chipped pavement and weedy lots and junk heaps, sardine canneries of corrugated iron, honky tonks, restaurants and whore houses, and little crowded groceries, and laboratories and flophouses." When Steinbeck's book *Cannery Row* was published in 1945, that year alone saw a quarter million *tons* of sardines hauled into Fisherman's Wharf by huge purse seiner vessels. It was all over by 1972, and Cannery Row became a popular tourist attraction. The original processing plants are now sites of restaurants, gift shops and boutiques.

On July 3, 1770, Captain Gaspar de Portola proclaimed Monterey the capital of Alta California, New Spain's northernmost province. Further inland, Portola built a primitive fort *(Presidio),* where most of Monterey's early homes were located. The old fort has vanished, but the early settlement's place of worship still remains. The **Royal Presidio Chapel** (bottom right), a small Spanish church vaguely Baroque in inspiration, was completed in the early 1790s.

Descendants of the original Spanish immigrants became known as *Californios,* and an upper class was created whose ranks were swelled by American and English businessmen. This group was destined to have an enduring influence on the serenely beautiful architecture unique to the Monterey Peninsula. Their homes were built either in the New England clapboard style (pictured above right), or in a form called Monterey adobe, a combination of Spanish/Mexican and New England colonial styles. These white-washed, mud-brick buildings have a Mediterranean flavor, expressed by terra cotta roofs, thick walls and carefully tended gardens. The Anglo Saxons added sloping roofs, pane windows, inside corridors and staircases.

CARMEL MISSION AND POINT LOBOS

After Captain Gasper de Portola completed his colonizing ceremony on a summer day in 1770, Father Junipero Serra blessed the construction of his second mission, one of a necklace of missions designed to convert Indian souls. De Portola and Serra soon clashed, however, prompting Serra to move his spiritual activity south to a lovely site in the Carmel Valley, where **Mission San Carlos Borromeo** came into existence in 1771. He is buried here, on the grounds of his favorite mission. The present church (left) was completed in 1797 from sandstone quarried in the nearby Santa Lucia mountains, and the architecture is a blend of influences from southern Mediterranean and North African countries. Unusual features include the fantastic star window, equivalent to the rose window in the European Gothic tradition, and the dome placed above the bell tower, instead of in its usual position over the main body of the church.

That **Point Lobos** (right) lends itself to the imagination is demonstrated by the fact that Robert Louis Stevenson used its topography as the background in *Treasure Island.* Artist Francis McComas once called Point Lobos "the greatest meeting of land and water in the world" and one can certainly see why. The area is distinguished by startling, craggy rock formations worn away by the sea to form small islands, inlets, and beach coves. Sea lions inhabit many of the outlying rocks. Their raucous barking gave the place its name, for the Spaniards called it "Punta de los Lobos Marinos," or "Point of the Sea Wolves." Just as it does along the 17-Mile Drive, the Monterey cypress clings tenaciously to cliffs since it needs a moist, cool sea breeze in order to live. The water off Point Lobos is cold and clean, and visitors are drawn to the exquisite handkerchief-size **Gibson Beach** and **China Cove;** the beauty of the latter is also enhanced by hanging gardens. Fortunately the area became part of the state park system in 1933.

Left, *the bell tower of* **Mission San Carlos Borromeo.** *Yes, this is really the Monterey Peninsula rather than Spain or North Africa as the architecture might suggest. Right, artist Francis McComas once called* **Point Lobos** *"the greatest meeting of land and water in the world."*

Top left, *the mountains plunge down to the sea in* **Big Sur.** *The sparsely-populated wild country, remains, in the words of Junípero Serra, "el pais grande del sur," (the big country of the south). Bottom left, the* **Bixby Creek Bridge.**

Above, *the* **Hearst Castle** *is an incongruous addition to the southern Big Sur coast.*

BIG SUR

"A walk on the wild side." This phrase from an old song aptly describes the 90-mile stretch of coastline from Carmel to San Simeon known as **Big Sur** (left). Here the Santa Lucia mountains meet the Pacific Ocean with breath-taking cliffs dropping as much as 1,000 ft. to the rocky shore. There are no villages or cities in Big Sur. Its natural beauty can be explored either on foot or by driving along the twists and turns of **Highway One**; camping is also popular. Completed in 1937, this road was declared the country's first Scenic Highway by Lady Bird Johnson in 1966.

The area has remained unspoiled throughout its history. Only a few pioneers arrived during the 1870s and 1880s, and they earned their living by mining or cutting redwood timber. Supplies had to be brought in by ship, so by 1889 the treacherous coastline was illuminated by the **Point Sur Lighthouse Station.** Another man-made addition to the landscape is the **Bixby Creek Bridge,** extending 714 ft. across the Bixby Canyon.

HEARST CASTLE

That money was no object in realizing a very special dream home is apparent immediately upon arrival at the **Hearst-San Simeon State Historic Park** (above). Familiarly known as "Hearst Castle," the grandiose structure is a monument to the ambition and taste of media tycoon William Randolph Hearst, whose life story was the prototype for the film *Citizen Kane.* Hearst referred to the property as "the ranch," which is what it was in the 19th century, when the vast acreage was acquired by his father, George Hearst. The family fortune came from the mines of Nevada and South Dakota, and William's mother, Phoebe Apperson, philanthropist, helped to endow the University of California. William Randolph Hearst, however, diverted the family's interest towards publishing. He learned the tricks of "yellow journalism" in New York, and went on to manage the *San Francisco Examiner,* numerous other newspapers, and later on, magazines, radio stations and movie studios.

Above, *the replica of a classical temple is opposite a magnificent outdoor swimming pool in the* **Hearst Castle.** Below, *Spanish/Moorish architecture was deliberately reproduced here at Hearst's own request.* Right, *a vista of the vast estate, located at* **San Simeon** *and now an historic park.*

Upon his father's death in 1919, Hearst decided to construct a palatial residence at San Simeon. He hired Julia Morgan — the first woman to earn a degree in engineering from U.C. Berkeley and a gifted architect who studied at Paris's Ecole des Beaux-Arts — to carry out his monumental scheme. Morgan worked from 1922 to 1947, when work on the estate was interrupted due to Hearst's final illness. The family gave the buildings, although not the surrounding property, to the state of California in 1958.

The facade of the principal building, *La Casa Grande,* is a facsimile of the cathedral in Seville, Spain. Built on the hillside are three guest houses, staircases, two swimming pools, a neo-classical theater, statuary, carefully landscaped gardens and terraces on what Hearst liked to call the *La Cuesta Encantada* (The Enchanted Hill). Hearst brought floors, ceilings, furniture and decoration over from European monasteries and castles, and elaborate reproductions filled in any gaps.

*The harbor at **Morro Bay,** halfway between San Francisco and Los Angeles.*

MORRO BAY AND SAN LUIS OBISPO

It is thought that the Portuguese explorer Juan Rodriguez Cabrillo first sighted the natural harbor of **Morro Bay,** and its sentinel, **Morro Rock,** (above right) in 1542. Sebastian Vizcaino and Gaspar de Portola, sailing under the Spanish flag, took note of the landmarks in 1602 and 1769 respectively. Morro Bay marks the beginning of the **South Central Coast,** a 200-mile stretch of Mediterranean-like shore down to Ventura. Morro Bay is protected by a slender peninsula, making it an ideal spot for fishing boats and pleasure craft to dock. The breakwater between the bay and the Pacific Ocean is composed of rocks, a pleasant place for blue heron and the peregrine falcon to perch. The area's dunes, salt marshes and lagoon have been set aside as a natural reserve, thus providing a sanctuary for many bird species, to the joy of many a bird-watcher. No hunting is allowed, although one can dig for clams. Golf courses and a natural history museum round out the list of sights in the reserve, officially designated as the **Morro Bay State Park.**

Although there are vast differences between the two, local residents like to think of **Morro Rock** as a Rock of Gibraltar in miniature. In actual fact, the Rock of Gibraltar is a limestone massif, while Morro Rock is the exposed summit of a plug dome volcano. The rock, an accumulation of lava flows, is one of the "Seven Sisters", a series of volcanic cones located between Morro Bay and San Luis Obispo. There are actually nine extinct volcanoes in the general vicinity, but two are not counted because one is completely submerged by water and the other one is not in visual line with the rest.

San Luis Obispo is now pronounced without a Spanish inflection, although its Spanish roots go back a long way. Situated twelve miles inland from Morro Bay, the town grew out of the mission founded by

*Once the site of a quarry, **Morro Rock** is actually an extinct volcano in the bay of the same name. A narrow, sandy strip joins Morro Rock to the mainland.*

Father Junipero Serra in 1772. The nearby volcanic peaks supposedly reminded the priest of a bishop's miter, so Serra called his mission "San Luis, Obispo (bishop) de Tolosa." Since the Chumash Indians would set the mission's thatched roof on fire during their attacks, a flame-resistant terra-cotta tile roof was finally substituted, setting a precedent to be widely followed in Californian architecture. The town's oldest homes are grouped around Mission Plaza, and include Victorian houses built by New England merchants who migrated here in search of business. The impact on the local culture made by the Spanish and the Native Americans as well as by the Anglo-Saxon settlers, is clearly explained in the **San Luis Obispo County Historical Museum.** Another reminder of an earlier era is the **Ah Louis Store,** in continuous operation since 1874. The old-fashioned general store was used by Chinese laborers brought in to work on the Southern Pacific Railroad as their meetingplace, post office and bank.

Revenue from livestock and agriculture has traditionally been the area's mainstay, and field crop production in addition to soil management are still popular courses of study at the **California Polytechnic State University,** although the school has also has an excellent reputation in the fields of computer science, engineering and architecture. The mixed farming and intellectual heritage, the town's distinctive feature, is most evident during the month of August, when San Luis Obispo county fair and annual Mozart festival take place. Both events pack in a crowd.

San Luis Obispo is exactly halfway between San Francisco and Los Angeles, so it should come as not surprise that the world's first motel was opened here in 1924. The word was coined as a contraction of "motor hotel"; unfortunately the original "Milestone Motel", later the "Motel Inn", burned down in 1989. Motel aficionados, however, can take heart by visiting the super-kitsch **Madonna Inn,** founded in 1959 by Alex Madonna, who even outrivals the singer/actress (no relation) in outrageousness. Rooms have comic strip themes.

The **Danish origin** of the first settlers is evident in **Solvang's architecture** and gift shops.

SOLVANG

South of San Luis Obispo along the coast is a 20-mile stretch of sand dunes divided into **Avila Beach** and **Pismo Beach,** a paradise for four-wheel-drive vehicles, swimmers, surfers, sunbathers and clam-diggers. Shell Beach, incorporated into the territory covered by Pismo Beach, offers a rocky coastline and a habitat for sea lions. The territory's volcanic origin is evident at the **Avila Hot Springs Resort.**

The California Central Coast has the peculiarity of mountains running from east to west instead of the more usual north to south direction. Backpackers and Sunday hikers have a selection of trails from which to choose in the nearby **Los Padres National Forest,** a reserve containing sections of the Santa Lucia, La Panza, San Rafael and Santa Ynez ranges.

Back towards the coast, **Lompoc,** California's flower garden, supplies many of the blossoms used in Pasadena's Rose Bowl Parade on New Year's Day. A flower festival is held in Lompoc every May. Also of interest is the **Mission La Purisima Concepcion** (the Immaculate Conception), the 11th mission in *El Camino Real,* the "royal road" from San Diego to Sonoma. The original 1787 mission, destroyed by an earthquake in 1812, was faithfully reconstructed — down to the convent, courtyard, olive mill, artisan workshops and corral— between 1813 and 1818.

The final stop on a tour before reaching Santa Barbara is the Danish settlement of **Solvang,** founded in 1911 by immigrants from...the Midwest! They called the settlement "Sunny Valley," and introduced the Danish clapboard architecture and windmills (left and above) so carefully maintained by their descendants. Picture-postcard-pretty Solvang is a tourist hangout, although the Scandinavian knick-knacks in the shop windows are genuine, as are the fabulous Danish pastries. The native dress, dance and theater are spotlighted during the **Danish Days** held every September. The tiny **Mission Santa Ines,** dating back to the early 1800s, is worth a stop-off as well.

Santa Barbara's strong Mediterranean influence is immediately visible in the **County Courthouse.**

SANTA BARBARA

The Spanish called this privileged area of the Central Coast *la tierra adorada,* "the beloved land," and **Santa Barbara** does appear to have been born under a lucky star. The city boasts a beautiful location between the sea and the Santa Ynez Mountains, a near-perfect climate, palm trees and even a **Yacht Harbor** (right). Spanish mission architecture completes the final touch on a Mediterranean-like setting. Santa Barbara was capital of the silent film industry: Charlie Chaplin had his studio and his home here, and Salvatore Ferragamo designed custom-made shoes for actresses before achieving international fame back in his native Italy. Today, the city has many exclusive residential enclaves, and stars such as Kevin Costner and Michael Douglas own private estates in the gently rolling hills of Montecito, south of Santa Barbara.

Who else lives in Santa Barbara? According to a local saying, "the newly wed and nearly dead" find the pleasant surroundings especially congenial. Through the ages, the town has even managed to turn natural disasters into events with some long-lasting, beneficial aspects. When much of Santa Barbara was leveled by the 1929 earthquake, city administrators decided to reconstruct everything in a Mediterranean style. One outstanding result of this urban plan is the **Santa Barbara County Courthouse** (above). The edifice vaguely looks like a 15th century Tuscan villa, ground floor window bars and all. Looking more closely, one discerns what appears to be the facade and rose window of a Spanish mission church, to which a neoclassical entrance has been added. The surprises, however, do not end there: the interior features Moorish tiles, as well as wooden ceilings and murals detailing the history of Santa Barbara County. The view from the clock tower looks out over other buildings, down to the sea.

The **Red Tile Walking Tour** starts at the Santa Barbara County Courthouse, and takes the visitor

Above and right, *Santa Barbara was an important port in the early days of its history. In fact, **Stearns Wharf** is the oldest dock on the West Coast. As well, the **Yacht Harbor** is a prominent feature of the waterfront.*

to the nearby **El Presidio de Santa Barbara State Historic Park.** Although Juan Rodriguez Cabrillo first sighted the area in 1542, it would not receive its name "St. Barbara, Virgin and Martyr" until 1602, when Sebastian Vizcaino dropped anchor offshore on the saint's feast day. Gaspar de Portola duly arrived in 1782 to construct a military stronghold, **El Presidio,** most of which was later destroyed in the 1812 earthquake. *El Cuartel,* the military barracks, and *La Caneda Adobe,* an officer's home, are holdovers, and everything else has been carefully reconstructed. Under Spanish, and later Mexican, rule, the society life of Alta California was considered to take place in Santa Barbara, much as politics and administration was confined to Monterey. This sense of exclusiveness was preserved by the first American settlers, who found ranching a profitable way of life. A fascinating glimpse into the colonial era is given by the nearby **Santa Barbara Historical Society Museum,** which conserves period clothing and artifacts in an adobe building.

Classical elements, including Ionic columns, are clearly evident on the facade of **Mission Santa Barbara.** The architect, a Franciscan father, drew his inspiration from a Spanish translation of a period text on ancient Roman architecture. Mission Santa Barbara is also the only one in California with two identical bell towers.

Father Junipero Serra may have blessed the Presidio, but he died before the original **Mission Santa Barbara** was completed in 1786. The earthquake of 1812 completely destroyed the mission, and it was rebuilt in 1820 in a serene Spanish High Renaissance/Moorish style (above). Known as "the Queen of the Missions", unusual features of the facade include Ionic columns and twin bell towers. Shades of yellow, orange and brown impart a feeling to the restrained Baroque style of the church's interior (right).

Next to the mission, the **Santa Barbara Museum of Natural History** and the **Santa Barbara Botanical Gardens** are certainly of interest to the visitor. The former has a vast collection of fossils, rocks and minerals, lithographs by the naturalist Audubon, as well as a plantarium and observatory. The museum also houses tools and ornaments of the local Chumash tribe, and a huge skelton of a blue whale. Over at the Botanical Gardens, one can take a break amidst the greenery of lawns, flowers, trees and

meadows, and even learn to appreciate the special beauty of cacti in a desert environment.

The oaks, pines and other evergreens native to the Central Coast have for the most part been replaced Santa Barbara by the palms and aromatic eucalyptus trees which have become a city trademark. The well-to-do can best afford Santa Barbara's sky-high real estate prices, though many others, attracted by the temperate climate and beautiful setting, would also like to live here. One could be even tempted to camp out under the foliage of the **Morton Bay Fig Tree.** California's largest and most ancient fig tree, planted in 1877, bears no fruit.

Moving from the theme of flora to that of fauna, the **Santa Barbara Zoological Gardens** is a favorite with children of all ages. Environmentalists will be glad to know that many of the animals had been sick or injured, and therefore it would have been difficult , if not impossible, for them to taken back to their natural habitats. Cormorants, herons and other sea birds nest in the saltwater marsh and lagoon of the **Andree**

Clark Bird Refuge. Pelicans, too, are often spotted at the **Stearns Wharf,** an historic site that has been in continuous operation since 1877. The pier is home to shops, restaurants and the occasional fisherman; what escapes their clutches is on display at the wharf's **Sea Center,** an aquarium of local marine life, operated under the auspices of the Santa Barbara Museum of Natural History.

Culture has its own special niche here, as well. Natives are especially proud of the **Santa Barbara Museum of Art,** housed in a traditional adobe building. The collection is a small yet wide-ranging one of pre-Christian sculptures, Egyptian art, French Impressionist and German Expressionist canvases, photography, American naif and Oriental art.

Santa Barbara's sandy, wide beaches are alluring, despite the incongruous view of oil derricks and off-shore drilling platforms in the distance. A nasty oil spill in 1969 damaged the ecosystem but has not succeeded in deterring the underwater extraction of petroleum. Despite the accident, the sea is clean today and has contributed to Santa Barbara's fame as a resort. The Channel Islands act as a natural breakwater to the Pacific waves, so the surface is placid enough although there are often strong undercurrents. Strangely enough, habit is such in Santa Barbara that city inhabitants and out-of-towners alike will sunbathe for hours on the beach, yet prefer to swim in one of the many available pools.

The **Scenic Drive** is a good way to tour Santa Barbara by car, and information on the route can be obtained at the visitor information center. A car is also needed to get to **University of California at Santa Barbara.** Driving inland one is reminded that the Central Coast is still ranch county, preserved for work, or, in the case of former president Ronald Reagan, for pleasure. Another reminder of the ranching heritage is the **Old Fiesta Days,** held in August.

The interior of **Mission Santa Barbara.** *Religious functions are still held here regularly as the mission has maintained its status of a parish church.*

Mission San Buenaventura is located right in the center of Ventura. The mission is named for a disciple of St. Francis of Assisi. The church interior exudes an intimate and inviting feeling, one heightened by the harmonious neoclassic altar.

VENTURA

Ventura has a definite Mediterranean flavor thanks to the shops and homes concentrated around the historic downtown area, not far from the port. Like many California towns, Ventura grew around its Roman Catholic settlement, **Mission San Buenaventura** (pictured to the left and above) and was actually named for it. The outpost was the last to be founded by Junipero Serra, and the pretty stucco church is all that is left of the complex after the destruction wrought by an earthquake in 1812. The simply designed structure was completed in 1782, and the brilliant white stucco facade does not prepare the visitor for the earth tones used in the interior, evident in the floor, oil paintings, and the Baroque-inspired statuary. Back outside, the surrounding gardens and the sound of water flowing in the nearby fountain accentuate a sense of peace.

Within walking distance of the church, the **Ortega Adobe** and the **Olivas Adobe** give the viewer a clear idea of how the Spanish settler of modest means (in the case of the former) or of unlimited means (in the case of the latter) made his home. More visual information about the colonial days is available at the **Ventura County Museum of History and Art.** That ranching and agriculture were fundamentally important to Ventura can be seen in the pioneer artifacts. Chumash Indian exhibits, dating back to 1500 B.C., are the focus of the **Albinger Archeological Museum,** which features a part of the ingenious aqueduct system constructed by the Spanish fathers to counter the water shortage.

Ventura traditionally makes a living from the produce of avocado, orange and lemon groves. Fine, sandy beaches — such as the **Point Mugu State Park** and **Buenaventura State Beach** — are only a stone's throw from the city center, and have aided the development of the tourist industry. There is something of interest on the beach for nearly everyone: sunbathers, surfers, boaters, fishermen, even hikers who can climb the neighboring hills.

*A small fleet of sailboats, motorboats and larger excursion boats dock in **Ventura harbor.***

***Ventura's broad, sand-filled beaches,** lined with palm trees, are an inviting sight.*

Visible on the horizon from Ventura's beaches are the **Channel Islands,** formed of solid volcanic rock. San Miguel, Santa Rosa, Santa Cruz, Anacapa and Santa Barbara are the separate links in the actual chain, united by a similar landscape and common marine life. The mountainous islands are covered with manzanita scrub, and steep bluffs drop sharply down to the sea. Safeguarded by the National Park System, the Channel Islands are home to numerous marine birds (such as the pelican), plant species, seals and sea lions. Sailboats often drop anchor close by to allow scuba divers to pry abalone, a seafood delicacy prized in California restaurants, from the ocean rocks.

Several of the Channel Islands are but a two-hour ferry ride away from Ventura. The starting point for an excursion is the Channel Island Visitors Center, a sure source of information on the archipelago's history, geological makeup, vegetation and sea life. The three islands comprising **Anacapa** can be visited all year long, while **Santa Barbara** can be reached only during the summer. Both offer camping, and sports enthusiasts can go hiking, swimming and snorkeling. Anacapa has the added enticements of an underwater shipwreck, visible to the scuba diver, and whale watching from January to March.

Santa Rosa is private property, although sail boats often hook up there so the crew can go fishing. Most of the archipelago is surrounded by giant underwater kelp forests, a natural habitat for bonito, yellowtail and other fish. There is occasional service to **Santa Cruz** from Santa Barbara, but **San Miguel** is off-limits to everyone. A little known fact is that Juan Rodriguez Cabrillo, who explored the coast under the Spanish flag in the mid-sixteenth century, is buried on San Miguel.

Another sort of paradise is located inland from Ventura. Unbeknownst to Jack London, the real "Valley of the Moon," at least according to its Chumash Indian name, is **Ojai,** the setting for the 1937 film *Lost Horizon.*

*In some respects, **Oxnard** resembles a New English fishing village, transplanted on the California coast.*

THE CENTRAL VALLEY AND OXNARD

There are two ways to get to L.A. from northern California. One is to drive through Bakersfield in the **Central Valley,** also known as the San Joaquin Valley. The Central Valley is where the desperate farm hands so poignantly depicted in *The Grapes of Wrath* migrated during the Depression days, contributing to an oversupply of labor. A series of aqueducts constructed in the 1940s in California's mountains irrigate the Central Valley, making the area far less than the desolate spot depicted in the Steinbeck classic. The flat landscape and the dry heat may be ideal for growing fruits and vegetables, yet traveling here is somewhat monotonous.

Besides cotton, wheat, table grapes (of which the Central Valley produces nearly a quarter of California's crop), the view outside the car window will include oil derricks as well. Oil was discovered here at the turn of the century, and replaced the dimishing gold resources as the area's primary resource next to agriculture. While traveling, turn on the car radio to hear the "Bakersfield sound," grass-roots country and western music made famous by native sons Merle Haggard and Buck Owens.

Bakersfield was christened by its founder, Colonel Thomas Baker, who cultivated the first local crops during the Civil War. A fire destroyed most of the frontier town in 1889; 50 buildings that survived the nineteenth century were later moved to the nearby 15 acre **Pioneer Village,** an open air historical spot worth a stop. Otherwise, the only reason to pull over would be to stroll through the old-fashioned **Bakersfield County Fair,** held in late August and early September.

If one would rather forego the Central Valley, the other choice is to steer straight for **Oxnard,** a pretty little town on the sea south of Ventura. Route 1 has the Santa Monica mountains as scenery, and Oxnard is a place to interrupt a journey in favor of a seafood dinner. The part of Oxnard near the dock resembles a New England fishing village, down to the

On the sign in the image: "*Absolutely* NO FISHING OR BIKE RIDING ON DOCKS"

lighthouse. Oxnard is primarily known for its fine, sandy beaches, a fact that belies the many farms in the vicinity specialized in produce such as strawberries. As a matter of fact, its name comes from a sugar beet refinery. A cultural note comes in at the **Carnegie Cultural Arts Center,** with its comprehensive art and archeological collections.

Moving closer to Los Angeles, the sand dunes give way to the rocky shoreline of **Point Mugu,** a naval base and wildlife reserve. Those with time on their hands and looking for something out of the ordinary can head to northern hills and the **Wheeler Hot Springs** for a thermal immersion in a natural setting. The **Sespe Condor Preserve** close by is the haunt of the super-protected, nearly-extinct California condor.

The Sespe preserve is part of the **Los Padres National Forest,** a vast region running parallel to the coast from Big Sur to south of Santa Barbara. It embraces several mountain ranges, canyons, and natural parks. The vegetation changes from oak groves and evergreens southward to brush and eucalyptus trees.

Pacific Ocean

MALIBU   HOLLYWOOD
SANTA MONICA   BEVERLY HILLS
VENICE   DISNEYLAND
LOS ANGELES

N
W   E
S

*Who wouldn't like to own a **beach cottage** in Malibu? The stars of the large and small screen discovered **Malibu** long ago, but then again, they can afford the local real estate prices.*

MALIBU

According to popular credo, surfers and surfers live in Malibu, which they do, of course, along with everyone else. The sun, sand, and sea-blessed community, however, arose from humble origins. The Chumash Indian residents called their home "Umalibo," and thus it remained until the territory was absorbed by a Spanish ranch in the early 19th century. The land was subsequently bought by an enterprising Irishman during the "Panic of 1857" for ten cents an acre, before passing title in 1887 to Frederick Hastings Rindge, who saw the beautiful setting — miles and miles of shore and the natural backdrop of the Santa Monica Mountains — as a potential "American Riviera." The uncompromising Mr. Rindge, and later on, his widow succeeded in keeping the paradise in the family until 1928. Hit hard by the Depression, Mrs. Rindge and her son began to sell some of the property, and the State of California financed the construction of the **Pacific Coast Highway**, then called Roosevelt Highway.

Stars of the silent film industry began to arrive in Malibu, and considerable development ensued. Nevertheless, this residential area today still does not offer the spectacle of high-rise buildings characteristic of some parts of the French and Italian Rivieras.

The bungalow is the typical Malibu home of many film employees and aficionados. Built as townhouses along the beach to ensure privacy, the **Malibu Beach Colony** has been described as a "Beverly Hills by the sea", without the shopping. A legacy of the past can be found in the **Adamson House,** once the Rindge mansion. Open to the public, the house has the beamed ceilings and ceramic tiles of a Mediterranean abode, along with a carefully landscaped garden. On the hills above the sea is **Pepperdine University,** and the position of this institute of higher learning allows a scenic view from its modern campus.

Now, the surfers. Protected by wet suits, they ride the ocean waves even in the winter. The visitor comes to Malibu to join the surfers on the many excellent beaches (above), whether to simply soak

Malibu is also a fisherman's paradise, starting from the **Malibu Pier.**

up the sun, or to go swimming, wind surfing, scuba diving, snorkeling, fishing and boating. The point of departure is the **Malibu Pier**, a favorite haunt of fishermen in search of perch, and of natives and visitors in search of a tasty seafood meal. Or, for those who wish to catch dinner with their bare hands, this possibility is afforded by grunion, a fish that regularly comes ashore to spawn when there is a full moon. Fishing considerations aside, a favorite haunt by the sea can be chosen from among the **Leo Carrillo State Beach, Zuma Beach, La Tunas State Beach, Corral State Beach,** the **Robert H. Meyer Memorial State Beaches** (comprising the El Matador, La Piedra and El Pescador beaches), **Westward Beach** and **Point Dume** (containing **Paradise Cove** as well as **Pirate's Cove,** preferred by nude bathers), **Surfrider Beach, Malibu Lagoon State Beach** and **Topanga State Beach.** Each beach has its own distinctive flair. The 1950s and 1960s surfing comedies were inspired by no other than Surfriders Beach, close to the pier, and the spot still seems a perfect place to play tried-and-true Beach

Boys songs. Malibu Creek flows into the Pacific Ocean at the **Malibu Lagoon State Beach,** where many bird species find the salt marsh and lagoon a congenial habitat. Stretching for miles and miles, popular **Zuma Beach** is especially spacious, while the rocky **Topanga State Beach** offers the chance to tour the nearby **Topanga Canyon State Park.**

Rock singers, the art crowd and New Age adherents were the original settlers of **Topanga Canyon** in the 1960s and '70s, and they were followed by big names in the entertainment industry such as Sylvester Stallone and Barbra Streisand. Their homes are beautiful although the surroundings are dry, desolate scrubland, familiar to millions as the background for many a made-for-TV movie. The state park covers miles of wilderness in the Santa Monica mountains, part of the Transverse Range, which cover a large area in California from east to west rather than the usual north to south direction. Finally, take a ride along **Mulholland Drive** for a breathtaking view of the coast from L.A. to Malibu.

THE J. PAUL GETTY MUSEUM

John Paul Getty was even more successful in the oil business as Randolph Hearst was in publishing, and outdid Hearst once again in construction of a remarkable California home open to visitors. While it can be said that Hearst's grand ambitions and lavish life style are typified by his "castle" at San Simeon, Getty brought history to life by re-creating a Herculaneum residence, Villa dei Papiri (destroyed by the eruption of Vesuvius in 79 B.C.) and filled it with many outstanding works of art. Getty especially loved the output of the Greek and Roman masters, Renaissance and Baroque painters, as well as neoclassical French furniture, furnishings and bric-a-brac. Getty died in 1976, two years after the museum bearing his name was inaugurated, but left such a generous endowment that its curators often buy masterpieces at the art world's major auctions. The museum houses the only documented painting in the country by the Italian Renaissance genius Masaccio, painstakingly-wrought illuminated manuscripts from the Middle Ages, beautifully decorated porcelain, crystal chandeliers, hand-woven tapestries in addition to canvases by Rembrandt, Rubens, Boucher and Gainsborough. Modern and contemporary photography, French impressionist works by Monet and others, plus Van Gogh's *Irises*, have extended the range of the exhibits.

The collection of sculpture from antiquity is especially strong, in keeping in tune with the scenario. Trees, flowers, shrubs and herbs like those that might have been grown 2,000 years ago at the Villa dei Papiri, which belonged to Julius Caesar's father-in-law, grow in the museum's interior and exterior gardens. The evocative surroundings are further enriched by bronze statues and modern casts of sculptures unearthed during the 18th century excavation of the villa (the originals are in Naples's Archeological Museum).

Since parking is limited, people wishing to come to the J. Paul Getty Museum must call in advance in order to make a reservation for their car, before savoring the sight of the many treasures housed in its galleries.

*Thanks to restricted parking, a visit to the spectacular and ever-growing art collection of the **J. Paul Getty Museum** is never marred by crowds.*

Santa Monica is perhaps the perfect embodiment of the California beach town.

PACIFIC PALISADES AND SANTA MONICA

Down the coast from Malibu, the traveler can come across two very different places of note in the Pacific Palisades: the **Self Realization Fellowship Lake Shrine** and the **Will Rogers State Historic Park** and **State Beach.** Paramahansa Yogananda, the Indian swami who introduced yoga to the United States, established an ecumenical place of worship near the bluffs overlooking the ocean before his death in 1954. A portion of Mahatma Gandhi's ashes are lovingly kept here.

Revered in his own way, Will Rogers represented the country's conscience in the simpler days before World War II. The cowboy-turned-comic was ever true to his country roots, as emphasized by a visit to the home in which he and his family lived between 1928 and 1935. An expert roper, Rogers had the ceilings raised in his house in order to practice more comfortably. The furnishings echo his ranch background, and there are hiking trails that can be followed for an enjoyable walk.

Santa Monica overlooks the Santa Monica Bay, and prior to the Civil War this stretch of prime beachfront belonged to the Southern Pacific Railroad Company. Railway officials had hoped to turn the area into a port for L.A. shipping, but were thwarted by the development of Wilmington to the south. Orange and lemon groves were planted instead, and the building of a streetcar linking Los Angeles to Santa Monica spurred the growth of the tiny community as a premier beach resort. This led to the building of the **Santa Monica Pier** (above) in 1908, subsequently declared a National Historic Landmark. Here part of the 1970s film hit *The Sting* was shot, and in a key scene Paul Newman was featured astride a brightly painted horse, part of a perfectly preserved merry-go-round from once a upon a time. Along the broadwalk are other old-fashioned amusements rarely found in cities these days, such as a beautiful carnival playground, bumper cars and arcades. A series of vintage black and white photos illustrates the history of Santa Monica, with special attention given to its beaches and boardwalk.

Another aspect of the past, when gambling ships were anchored in the bay, was vividly brought to life by novelist Raymond Chandler, who disguised Santa Monica under the pseudonym "Bay City." With his popular and cynical sleuth Philip Marlowe as the leading character, these books were, and continue to be, widely read. The fledging aviation industry also

The **Santa Monica Pier** *is a wonderland for children of all ages thanks to its carousel and other authentic rides and amusements from the early part of the 20th century. Bottom photo, the front of a café on the pier provides a strong visible reminder of the murals which decorate the town's most prominent places.*

made its home in Santa Monica during the early 20th century, and production by the original Douglas Aircraft Company can be viewed at the **Museum of Flying** near the municipal airport.

With the opening of the Santa Monica Freeway in 1966, allowing quick accessibility to L.A., both the resident population and number of visitors grew at a speedy rate. "Laid-back" came to be an expression epitomizing the way of life in Santa Monica, with its pedestrian-friendly downtown. Many people use their car as method of transportation here, yet an equal number can be seen walking, bicycling and getting around on roller skates or by skateboard.

Another element of Santa Monica and its neighbor Venice, are the **murals** adorning the most unexpected places in a blaze of color.

*Body building, roller skating, selling or simply providing entertainment: people in Venice make a point of conducting their lives out of doors, preferably on the **Ocean Front Walk.***

Following pages: *a familiar sight, thanks to the made-for-TV movie, is the imposing, modern **L.A. skyline.** Until the 1950s, when construction methods ensured the skyscrapers could withstand earthquakes, the tallest building was **City Hall** (on the horizon, far right).*

VENICE

Venice is, and has always been, "far-out". It can be best described as a 24-hour revolving circus, and the leading characters are always on the move, whether it be on roller blades (the craze originated here), roller skates, skateboards or, lifting weights on **Muscle Beach** in the hope of emulating Arnold Schwarzengger. Strolling street musicians and stand-up comedians provide nonstop entertainment as well. Most of the action takes place on the distinctive **Venice Boardwalk,** stretching two miles along the famous Ocean Front Walk, home to a variety of shops and street vendors. In the '50s Venice was a pole of attraction for the beat generation, followed by hippies and rock stars such as Jim Morrison and the Doors in the '60s and early '70s. The avant-garde art scene is well represented by Venice's numerous galleries and street murals. Consonant with the local lifestyle is the town's distinctive open-air sculpture (above), meant to symbolize the concept of freedom.

The community has undergone a series of changes since the beginning of the century, when developer and manufacturer Abbot Kinney founded Venice with the intent of recreating its Italian namesake on the shores of the Pacific Ocean. Thanks to his vision, reclamation of the Santa Monica swamps took place, and a 16-mile network of **canals** was subsequently built, complete with bridges and romantic gondolas. The St. Mark's, an Italianate rococo hotel was constructed, and silent screen star Mae Murray adhered to the neighborhood's concept by building a Venetian-style *palazzo*. Sadly, the discovery of oil put an end to the real-life stage set. Oil-drilling rigs and platforms menaced the quaint area, and spills menaced the canals' limpid waters. Most of the waterways were filled in, although a portion of the Grand Canal and the adjacent homes and other edifices were spared, and can still be seen today.

It is chic again to live in Venice, and to visit the trendy restaurants and art galleries. The renaissance continues here, in its own extremely personalized way.

 *LOS ANGELES*

 Love it or hate it: Los Angeles is too large and too complex a city to inspire ambivalent feelings.

Contrary to popular belief, which defines L.A. as little more than a sum of suburbs, the city does have a heart, distinguished by glass, steel and stone skyscrapers (above). Downtown Los Angeles is roughly delineated by Temple Street to the north, Olympic Boulevard to the south, and Alameda and Figueroa respectively to the east and west. Considered the smallest of any major American city, the city center still reflects L.A.'s remarkable urban variety through the kaleidoscope of its mini-districts.

Historically, Los Angeles began in and around **Olvera Street,** but later development pushed the heart of the city to another area, approximately seven blocks west, on **Pershing Square.** But when the fear of earthquakes inspired city planners to prohibit buildings more than 150 ft. high, many companies began to move out to **Wilshire Boulevard** (a stretch going all the way to the Pacific Ocean) and other outlying areas. Thanks to new developments in building techniques, the old ban on tall edifices was finally revoked in 1957, leading to a construction boom in central L.A. which peaked during the 1980s. Today, the visitor can admire the majestic downtown skyscrapers. It is a spectacle not to miss, particularly at sunset, when the last rays of light coming from the ocean illuminate the polished surfaces. Equally well known is **Dodger Stadium,** (pictured on page 120, top), home base of the L.A.

Dodgers baseball team. For the visitor who happens to be in Los Angeles during clear winter days, the beauty of the skyline is heightened by the snow-covered San Gabriel mountains in the background.

L.A. of course means freeways (see top photo, left, page 124). Although downtown is served by mini-buses (DASH), taxis, and more recently by the Red Line subway, the best way to enjoy the city's attractions is by foot. Leave the car behind and walk instead; a full tour will take from four to five hours.

Starting from **Pershing Square,** which provides several levels of underground parking, one can visit the **International Jewelry Center** on the southeast corner of Hill and Sixth Street. The way this modern structure has been built allows jewelers to take advantage of northern light, supposedly the best in which to examine fine gems. More shops and offices of the city's large jewelry trade can be found one block down on Hill Street. Always in the same district, at 61 Olive Street, is the **Oviatt Building,** one of most important examples of Art Deco architecture found within Los Angeles city limits, and once a prestigious clothing shop boasting such clients as

Rudolph Valentino and Douglas Fairbanks Jr. Not to be missed is the entryway, created by French jeweler and glassware designer René Lalique. The store was replaced by today's **Rex II Restaurant,** decorated as an 1920s ocean liner in keeping with the overall Art Deco decor.

North of Olive, between Sixth and Fifth streets is the prime location of the **Biltmore Hotel,** completed in 1923. A recent renovation has brought back the splendor of the its wooden beam ceilings and Spanish-inspired architecture. The central staircase, complemented by a wrought iron balustrade, leads up to the Galleria level and the Music Room, Gold Room and Grand Ballroom.

East Street can be reached by going through the hotel, and then the **Los Angeles Central Library.** The library is housed in the Goodhue Building, named after its designer Bertram Goodhue, and is a 1926 tower topped by a pyramid-shaped roof. The overall architecture, including the sculptures at the base and inscription, all reflect the theme "the light of learning." Despite damage wrought by arson in the 1980s, the Central Library is the country's third

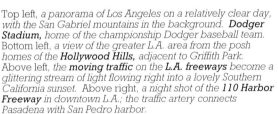

Top left, *a panorama of Los Angeles on a relatively clear day, with the San Gabriel mountains in the background.* **Dodger Stadium,** *home of the championship Dodger baseball team.* Bottom left, *a view of the greater L.A. area from the posh homes of the* **Hollywood Hills,** *adjacent to Griffith Park.* Above left, *the* **moving traffic** *on the* **L.A. freeways** *become a glittering stream of light flowing right into a lovely Southern California sunset.* Above right, *a night shot of the* **110 Harbor Freeway** *in downtown L.A.; the traffic artery connects Pasadena with San Pedro harbor.*

largest library, containing 1,900,000 books, 10,000 magazines and over 2 million historic photographs.

From there, the visitor's tour leads to a plaza formed by the twin **Atlantic Richfield (ARCO) Towers,** a huge shopping mall and a 52-story office complex, also home to the **Los Angeles Visitor and Convention Bureau** as well as Herbert Bazer's stair-shaped sculpture **Double Ascension.** An outside escalator conducts one up to a pedestrian bridge over 5th Street and to the **Westin Bonaventure Hotel,** made up of cylinders covered with thousands of dark glass panes. The futuristic structure is noted for its six-level open courtyard, glass capsule elevators and revolving restaurant on the main top floor. Across Fourth Street is the **World Trade Center,** an enclosed mall occupying several blocks. Another footwalk connects to the 52-story **Bank of America Building** and to the series of plazas, gardens and skyscrapers comprising **Bunker Hill.**

The 74-story high **First Interstate World Center** can be admired on the southern part of the hill. The building is flanked by two other giants. To the east is the **Gas Company Tower;** to the west, the **444 Plaza Building,** best known to the general public as the venue of the *L.A. Law* TV series. The corner of 4th and Hope Streets is a good place to view two modern sculptures, **Ulysses** by Alexander Liberman and **Mind, Body and Spirit** by Gidon Graetz. A tour of the area would not be complete without a stop-off at the **wells Fargo Center,** modeled after a glass-walled Victorian greenhouse, in addition to the twin-towered **California Plaza.** The last addition to the plaza is situated on Grand Avenue. There, a distinctive red sandstone edifice signals one's arrival at the **Museum of Contemporary Art (MOCA),** dubbed as a "private museum with a public conscience," when it was founded in 1979.

Inaugurated in 1986, MOCA hosts both special

exhibitions and a permanent collection comprised of over 600 paintings, drawings, sculptures and other media covering major artistic movements from the 1940s to the present. Especially well represented are Abstract Expressionism, Pop Art and Minimal Art, with works by Jackson Pollock, Joan Miró, Alexander Calder, Mark Rothko, Robert Rauschenberg, Franz Kline and Alberto Giacometti. In the not-so-distant future, MOCA itself, built according to specifications by Japanese architect Arata Isozaki, may be classified on the same artistic level as its avant-garde masterpieces of the recent past.

Since MOCA was not completed in time for the 1984 Olympics, a former warehouse in L.A.'s Little Tokyo was adapted into the so-called **Temporary Contemporary** museum (N. Central Avenue). As a site of changing exhibitions, it proved to be so popular that it still is an operating branch of MOCA today.

Back to the Bunker Hill area, the performing arts are the domain of the **Music Center,** domicile of the Joffrey Ballet, the Los Angeles Philharmonic Orchestra and the Civic Light Opera. The Music Center is composed of the **Dorothy Chandler Pavilion,** the **Ahmanson Theatre** and the **Mark Taper Forum** around a plaza marked by a Jacques Lipschitz sculpture and fountain. The Dorothy Chandler Pavilion, familiar to millions as the site of the Academy Awards extravaganza, needs little introduction, although few may know that opera and symphonic concerts are performed there as well. The Ahmanson Theatre specializes in comedies and musicals, while the Mark Taper Forum concentrates on drama and the premiere of new plays.

A tour of downtown Los Angeles wouldn't be complete without going to see the nearby **Civic Center,** a cluster of public buildings including the Parker Center (headquarters of the L.A. police department), the Federal Courthouse, the Criminal Courts Building, the Federal Courthouse Building, the Hall of Records, and last but not least, **City Hall.** Shaped like a Crayola crayon, City Hall was erected in 1926, and the citizens of Los Angeles voted to allow the building to rise to a then-prohibitive 27 stories. Architecturally speaking, City Hall combines neo-classical and Egyptian elements in a distinctive facade known to the viewers of *Dragnet* and *Superman.* The lookout on the top floor offers an excellent perspective of downtown Los Angeles, either visible in all its glory, or shrouded in smog.

Who says L.A. has no culture? A trip down Wilshire Boulevard leads one to Hancock Park and the **Los Angeles County Museum of Art** (LACMA), consisting of several buildings clustered around the Times-Mirror Central Court. The Japanese Pavilion contains one of most exhaustive groupings of

Top left, **Los Angeles City Hall.** *Built in the 1920s, it is often used as a film location.* Bottom left, *the* **Jacques Lipchitz sculpture** *dedicated to peace signals one's arrival to the* **Music Center.** *Behind the sculpture is the Department of Water and Power building.* Top right, *"**Double Ascension,"** a sculpture by Herbert Bazer in the* **ARCO Plaza,** *where the Los Angeles Visitor and Convention Bureau is located.* Bottom right, **444 Plaza Building.**

Japanese art in the world, from silk screens and parchments to paintings, sculptures and ceramics. In the Ahmanson Building, the emphasis is on Indian, Oriental and pre-Columbian artifacts, works from medieval and Renaissance Europe, in addition to textiles and costumes from a variety of civilizations.

Next door, be careful not to get stuck in the **La Brea Tar Pits.** Since the beginning of the century, paleontologists discovered fossil remains and skeletons of animal, plant and bird species dating back to the Pleistocene epoch (Ice Age) in the murky, black pits. These are conserved at the nearby **George C. Page Museum of La Brea Discoveries.**

Top row (left), *commercial buildings and residential homes seem small in comparison to this **freeway intersection** just south of downtown L.A. Right, the Security Pacific National Bank Building is behind the sculpture **"Ulysses"** by Alexander Liberman.*

Second row (left), *a **pedestrian bridge** coming out of the World Trade Center. A regular feature of downtown L.A., pedestrian bridges allow one to pass from one block to another without setting foot on the street. Right, the **444 Plaza Building,** with the First World Interstate Center in the background.*

Bottom row (left), *a huge street sculpture celebrating **car traffic,** one of L.A.'s inescapable features, by the **Wells Fargo Center.** Right, one of the two **ARCO towers.***

Top right, *from Grand Avenue up to the sky (from the left) the **Wells Fargo Center, IBM,** and the twin **ARCO towers.***

Bottom right, *the sculpture **"Mind, Body and Spirit"** by Gidon Graetz between the Wells Fargo Center and the Great Western Bank Building.*

Los Angeles is a multicultural city par excellence, and nowhere is this more evident than in **Chinatown, Little Tokyo** and the **El Pueblo de Los Angeles State Historic Park.**

Colorful pagodas signal one's arrival in **Chinatown**, a copy-in-miniature of the famed San Francisco district. Chinese New Year is celebrated here too, and dim sum brunch regularly draws a crowd of foreigners. Many Chinese have moved to L.A. suburbs as they have become more upwardly mobile, and their place has been taken in large part by the Vietnamese, who add their own distinctive note.

Tempera and sushi are the order of the day in **Little Tokyo**, a stone's throw from City Hall. The Japanese art of flower arranging is also on display, as is Japanese art and Kabuki theater.

El Pueblo de Nuestra Senora La Reina de Los Angeles was founded in 1781, and what little is left of the 19th century Spanish/Mexican settlement is conserved in the state historic park.

Avila Adobe dates back to 1818, and **Our Lady, Queen of the Angels** has been a continuously-operating parish church since that time.

Top, *the entrance to the* **Mandarin Plaza** *in* **Chinatown.** *The traditional gate welcomes visitors to a collection of shops and restaurants.* Middle photo, **Japanese Village Plaza** *in* **Little Tokyo,** *where one can find many authentic Japanese restaurants and stores.* Bottom photo, **Olvera Street** *keeps alive the Mexican traditions in the oldest part of the city.*

Several places of interest immediately outside downtown Los Angeles are **Union Station, Exposition Park,** and **Griffith Park** and **Observatory.**

L.A.'s original Chinatown was evicted and moved to its present location in order to make way for **Union Station,** the L.A. train station, completed in 1939. No expense was spared in the sumptuous interior decoration. After a brief heyday as a busy railroad terminal, this modern Mission-style building has faded into little more than a tourist attraction.

The 1932 and 1984 Olympics were held, among other places, in the **Los Angeles Memorial Coliseum** at Exposition Park, also home to the **Los Angeles County Museum of Natural History.**

Nestled in the Santa Monica Mountains, **Griffith Park** allows the urban dweller to wander along miles of hiking trails, visit the animals in their natural environment at the **L.A. Zoo,** investigate the night sky at the **Observatory,** and to see the celestial displays of the **Planetarium.**

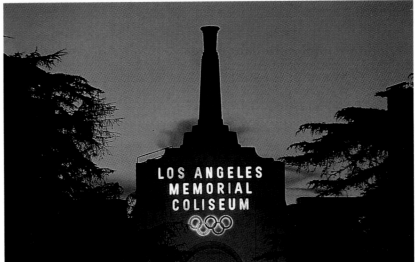

Top, *Union Station is L.A.'s train connection to the rest of the country.* Middle, *home to two Olympics, innumerable athletic competitions and live concerts, the architecture of the* **Los Angeles Memorial Coliseum** *is inspired by Rome's Coliseum.* Bottom, *the Griffith Observatory and Planetarium in* **Griffith Park,** *the largest urban wilderness area in the United States.*

Left, *dreams of stardom begin by gazing at the* **world-famous Hollywood sign,** *overlooking the city from the summit of Hollywood Hills.* Above, *main entrance to* **Mann's Chinese Theater** *on Hollywood Boulevard.* Right, *screen stars aspire to be immortalized in the* **Hollywood Walk of Fame.** Bottom, *one by one, eminent members of the movie industry have left their* **personal messages, hand** *and* **footprints** *outside Mann's (formerly Grauman's) Chinese Theater.*

HOLLYWOOD

Much in the manner of a fading film star, **Hollywood** lives on dreams of ancient glory, just as Gloria Swanson did in *Sunset Boulevard.* The entrance to Paramount Studios, featured in a crucial scene of the 1950s film classic is still there, and the movie-making giant is the only big name found in Hollywood, along with CBS television.

Seduced by the lingering aura of the old days, the tourists keep coming to pay homage to the old, familiar landmarks. Hollywood's reputation was once as big as the **Hollywood sign** (left) in the neighboring hills. Keeping in step with the fantasies spun by Hollywood, the tall letters, put up in 1923 to advertise a nearby housing development, originally spelled out "Hollywoodland."

In light of all this, it is hard to believe that Hollywood was an aggregation of farms at the turn of the century, before becoming incorporated into the city of Los Angeles in 1910. Future movie moguls Cecil B. DeMille and Samuel Goldwyn arrived shortly thereafter and eventually created the "star system,"

Above, a **mural on Hollywood Boulevard** portraying important figures in the history of American cinema. Bottom photo, a **Tyrannosaurus rex** atop "Ripley's Believe It or Not Odditorium" threatens passersby walking along Hollywood Boulevard at the Highland intersection.

a seemingly glamorous way of life which contributed in its own way to the Hollywood legend.

Although the stars are gone, many have left their mark in the courtyard of **Mann's Chinese Theater**, formerly **Grauman's Chinese Theater.** In 1927, Sid Grauman built what could be considered a stage set for a Chinese film (p. 129) in order to screen movie premieres guaranteed to draw the attractive, well-dressed "in" crowd. Legend has it that he stumbled across freshly-laid concrete during the inauguration of the not-fully-completed theater, and came up with the idea of asking the movie crowd to create a similar lasting impression. Ever since then, screen gods and goddesses of the moment are invited, one by one, to leave their imprints and

signature (p. 129) in wet cement.
Mann's Chinese Theater is located on Hollywood Boulevard, as is the **Hollywood Walk of Fame,** consisting of famous names engraved in brass on a pink star inlaid in a stone mosaic panel (p. 129). In this case, the stars or their affiliated studios had to pay for this privilege.

Another must-see on a tour of Hollywood is the **Capitol Records Building** on North Vine Street. One may not immediately grasp that the edifice is meant to resemble a stack of records topped by a phonograph needle (bottom right). Nat King Cole and Bobby Mercer came up with the novel idea, and the singer is depicted in a mural out front.

Top photo, *the newest development on Hollywood Boulevard, next to Mann's Chinese Theater, is a movie theater complex called the* **Hollywood Galaxy.** Middle photo, *cruising in Hollywood.* Bottom photo, *a fire explodes in a Far Western town - right in front of your eyes. Not to worry. This 'controlled' piece of fiction can be enjoyed at the Wild, Wild, Wild West Stunt Show, one of the many forms of entertainment for the visitors of "movie worlds", all part of the Universal City Studios Tour.*

BEVERLY HILLS

West of Hollywood, the neon signs of Sunset Boulevard (a.k.a. the Sunset Strip) disappear as the road crosses **Beverly Hills,** one of the nation's most exclusive neighborhoods. Ordinary mortals dream of living in this modern day Nirvana, a perfectly ordered world of careful landscaping and houses big enough to qualify for the term "mansion." An aerial view of the small city (pop. 34,000) so proudly independent from Los Angeles reveals what could be the highest pro capita concentration of palm trees, swimming pools and tennis courts in the country. And yet the recent history of Beverly Hills began right on the unglamorous Sunset Boulevard.

Beans were the chief crop of the area's farmland at the turn of the century, and real estate developers despaired of interesting anyone in acquiring property until one developer had the brilliant idea of building the **Beverly Hills Hotel** in 1912. Big names in the movie industry quickly turned 9641 Sunset Boulevard into one of the classiest addresses in town. Many a film deal (and other sorts of deals) would be clinched in the hotel's **Polo Lounge,** and the bungalows on the property soon became a "home away from home" for many a star. But that's getting ahead of the story.

From 1919 onwards, Douglas Fairbanks and Mary Pickford held court in their mansion **Pickfair,** above the Beverly Hills Hotel, and until their divorce in the 1930s, up-and-coming stars knew that they had finally "made it" when a dinner invitation from Pickfair arrived. A host of silent screen names moved into the neighborhood, followed by movie celebrities of successive eras. Mary Pickford remained in her home until her death in 1979, and Pickfair was sold to the owner of several L.A. pro sports teams.

Of course, one of the main reasons people come to Beverly Hills is to go star-gazing, to see where Marlene Dietrich lived and where Marilyn Monroe and Joe DiMaggio honeymooned. Equipped with maps sold at street corners, visitors will probably have better luck viewing where the stars of the past resided rather than actually seeing the closely-guarded stars of the present.

Of course, the rich and famous *do* come out sometime, to go...shopping on **Rodeo Drive,** part of the **Golden Triangle district** bordered by Little Santa Monica, Crescent Drive and Wilshire Boulevard. The most recent development is **Two Rodeo Drive,** probably one of the most expensive shopping complexes ever built — its original cost came to $130 million. One can browse in its exclusive boutiques and salons in a European-style setting of cobblestone streets, elegant steps and an Italianate square. If shopping for high fashion clothing or jewelry is not someone's primary interest, each avenue of the Golden Triangle abounds with exquisite art galleries, antique shops and picturesque restaurants.

Left, *aerial view of the mansions, manicured lawns, swimming pools and tennis courts of* **Beverly Hills.** Top right, *wheeling and dealing within the entertainment industry traditionally occurs at the Beverly Hills Hotel.* Bottom right, **Royce Hall** *on the* **UCLA campus** *in nearby Westwood.*

CENTURY CITY

The group of high-rise buildings next to Beverly Hills is the business community of **Century City,** an offshoot of **Twentieth Century Fox Pictures.** Century City grew out of the studio giant's back lot, and as could be expected, most of the commercial activity here is movie-related. Back in the heyday of the star system, when Twentieth Century Fox was producing such Oscar-winning films as *Gentleman's Agreement* and *All About Eve,* a veritable plethora of famous actors and actresses were chauffeured to work daily at studio headquarters. **The Hollywood Experience,** an hour-long multimedia show headquartered in Century City, takes the viewer back to this era. And, of course, there was no end to the fancy cars that the stars (and other Californians) owned in an area dedicated to the cult of the automobile, a fact that has inspired an exhibition called **The Road Show.**

Other notable Century City landmarks include the **ABC Entertainment Center Complex,** the twin tower **Century Plaza Hotel** as well as the **Schubert Theater.** Tourists will also be delighted by the variety of offerings in the **Century City Shopping Center** and **Marketplace,** featuring 140 shops, an international food section and a 14-screen movie theater. Another interesting newcomer is the Simon Wiesenthal Center's **Museum of Tolerance** on Pico Boulevard, providing an in-depth look at racism and prejudice in the modern world. Hands-on exhibits encourage the visitor to see the world through the eyes of others as they explore 20th century wars, genocide and oppression, including the Holocaust.

*Film and TV-related activity on a day-to-day basis takes place in **Century City,** where the studios of **Twentieth Century Fox** have always been located.*

*Welcome to the **Magic Kingdom.***

DISNEYLAND

No one is as instantly recognizable throughout the world as **Mickey Mouse,** host of the one and only **Disneyland.** Nearly as familiar a sight is the turreted **Sleeping Beauty Castle,** another visual symbol of what was intended to be, according to its founder Walt Disney, the "happiest place on earth."

For the more than 10 million people who come here annually, this is exactly what Disneyland represents. In steady expansion since its inauguration in 1955, the enormous theme park ranks as the single top attraction in the state of California today. One proof of its popularity: the parking lot occupies double the space of all of Disneyland's attractions!

It's hard to believe that the area was first settled by German immigrants, who named the town **Anaheim,** or "house over the Santa Ana river," and harder still to envisage Walt Disney contemplating acres of nearby orange groves as the site of his future **theme lands,** eight in all. **Main Street U.S.A.** is the starting point, a nostalgic homage to turn-of-the-century small town life. At the **Disneyland Opera House** one can enjoy *Great Moments With Mr. Lincoln,* an introduction to the American president featuring a combination of special audio effects and animation. After sunset from Spring to September (weekends only) there is the **Main Street Electrical Parade,** followed by the **Fantasy in the Sky** fireworks display.

Fantasyland draws heavily on the Walt Disney films *Peter Pan* and *Snow White,* in addition to such classics from children's literature as *The Wind in the Willows* and *Alice in Wonderland.* Even the Abominable Snowman is on hand, waiting to meet people after a thrilling **Matterhorn Bobsled** ride down a snowcapped mountain.

The Swiss Family Treehouse, Jungle Cruise and the *Enchanted Tiki Room* are among the chief entertainments of **Adventureland,** while **New Orleans Square** re-creates an authentic rough-and-tumble Creole atmosphere around the town's distinctive buildings. Mississippi steamboats and Wild West towns create the setting for **Frontierland,** and *Space Mountain* allows one to become an astronaut in **Tomorrowland.**

Pacific Ocean

DEATH VALLEY
NATIONAL MONUMENT

ANTELOPE VALLEY

LOS ANGELES

N
W E
S

*The **orange poppy**, California's state flower, thrives in the **Antelope Valley**, also the site of many flight experiments conducted by Chuck Yeager and other pilots from the end of World War II to the present.*

ANTELOPE VALLEY

In complete contrast to L.A., nature reigns in the **Antelope Valley.** Here, after the San Gabriel Mountains, the Mojave Desert begins. The barren landscape is enlivened in the springtime by acres upon acres of orange poppies, California's official state flower, in bloom along with other colorful wildflowers (above). The sight is impressive enough to draw carloads of Angelenos (as the natives of Los Angeles call themselves) and visitors to the **California Poppy Preserve.** Fruit orchards also thrive in the dry heat of Antelope Valley, and summer and early fall is the time to drive around the area in search of freshly-picked cherries, peaches, pears and apples. Agriculture, too, is the keynote of the late August **Antelope Valley Fair** and **Alfalfa Festival.**

Sadly, antelopes have been extinct in the valley since the late 19th century. Their favorite haunts were threatened by the arrival of railroad tracks in addition to farms, ranches and a myriad of small towns such as **Palmdale** and **Lancaster.** What has

survived, to the delight of environmentalists, is the rare desert tortoise, easy to spot in Antelope Valley's **Desert Tortoise Natural Area,** an excellent place to go hiking along the marked trails. Those in search of natural wonders should head for the **Devil's Punchbowl County Park.** The steep-walled gorge was created in part by the shifting of the nearby San Andreas and San Jacinto faults.

Antelope Valley once had its own gold rush, as attested by the presence of the abandoned **Tropico Gold Mine.** Another dream that went bust is **Shea's Castle,** built in the 1920s by the entrepreneur of the same name. The edifice, based on an authentic Irish castle, was abandoned when the owner lost his fortune and ended his life during the 1929 Wall Street crash.

Near perfect weather has contributed to the popularity of hot air balloon ascents in a place where the first jet airplane also was tested. Thus, it is not by chance that Antelope Valley is home to **Edwards Air Force Base,** the nation's second largest flight installation and the site of many aerospace experiments.

Above, *the corrugation of the landscape in* **Death Valley** *is due to volcanic activity. Right, the deep and arid desert basin was named by a group of prospective gold miners who crossed it in 1849. Beside dunes, Death Valley has numerous salt and alkali flats, colorful rock formations, desert plants, small animal life and footprints of prehistoric animals.*

DEATH VALLEY

Few places in the world have captured the imagination quite like the **Death Valley National Monument.** It is a geologist's living laboratory — as well as the hottest place on earth.

Death Valley was formed millions of years ago. Volcanic activity caused mountains to rise, and the valley floor subsequently became a giant lake. Evaporation left behind the salt flats for which Death Valley has become famous, and the sand dunes seem to extend beyond the horizon. Summer temperatures hover around 120° F.

Mineral deposits have colored the **Artist's Palette,** while the brown, eroded hills of **Zabriskie Point** furnished the setting for the 1970 Michelangelo Antonioni film. Not far away is the **Devil's Golf Course,** seemingly made to order out of pure salt. The panorama from **Dante's View** takes in **Badwater,** a saline pond with the distinction of being the lowest point (282 ft. below sea level) in the entire Western Hemisphere, a decided contrast to Death Valley's highest point, **Telescope Peak** (11,000 ft.).

Pacific Ocean

LOS ANGELES

LONG BEACH HUNTINGTON BEACH PALM SPRINGS

NEWPORT BEACH JOSHUA TREE N.M.

PALM DESERT

*A panorama of Long Beach Harbor. The **Queen Mary.***

THE PALOS VERDES PENINSULA AND LONG BEACH

Steep bluffs overlooking the ocean guard access to the exclusive neighborhood of the **Palos Verdes Peninsula.** The name means "green trees" in Spanish, and the territory has remained relatively unspoiled, the domain of ranch homes, golf courses and riding stables. In harmony with the surroundings is the **Wayfarer's Chapel,** designed in the late 1940s by Lloyd Wright, the famous architect's son, and completed in 1951. The glass-and-wooden-beam structure was meant to evoke the philosophy of Emmanuel Swedenborg, the 18th century mystic, mathematician and scientist from Sweden. "God's Candle," a brightly illuminated cross at the summit of the chapel, can be seen for miles out at sea.

Further down the coast, the seaport of **San Pedro** provides a counterpoint to the elegance of the Palos Verdes Peninsula. The varied ethnic backgrounds of the sailors who settled here has contributed to the lively mix of residents and local cuisine. Of note is the **Cabrillo Marine Museum,** a modern edifice near Cabrillo Beach, designed by Frank Gehry. The museum's 35 aquariums allow a close observation of marine mammals and fish that thrive in the Pacific Ocean waters.

After San Pedro is **Long Beach,** California's premier port, ranking seventh nationwide in terms of overall shipping and handling. Long Beach was founded as a resort in the 19th century, and was thus christened to advertise the beauty of its sandy shores. A farsighted developer promoted a rail link to Los Angeles at the turn of the century, and Long Beach underwent a boom, fueled by the discovery of petroleum.

Long Beach's destiny seems inextricably linked to transportation. McDonnell-Douglas Aircraft opened here, and the maiden (and only) flight of the **Spruce Goose** took place in the skies above the city harbor in 1947. The federal government had commissioned Howard Hughes to build the *Spruce Goose* to aid the

Long Beach *has maintained the lovely five miles of shoreline for which it was christened*

war effort. The statistics pertaining to the birch (not spruce, as one Congressman called it in derision) hydroplane are nothing short of monumental: weighing 400 tons, the eight-story-high vehicle could convey 750 soldiers and several tanks to their destination. The wingspan alone is more than 300 ft. Until early 1993, the *Spruce Goose* was housed in the world's largest hangar along with mementos of Hughes and his aviation and film career. The giant aircraft is currently found in Oregon.

The **Queen Mary** is on Pier J. No expense was spared in the construction of this 1930s luxury liner, a fact important to the city fathers who purchased the boat during the 1960s. As they had foresaw, the *Queen Mary* quickly became a prime Long Beach tourist attraction, and people line up to walk around the decks and engine rooms as well as to admire the sumptuous furnishings of the ballroom and staterooms.

Always on the theme of transportation, gondolas are one of the ways to get around **Naples,** a Long Beach neighborhood built on canals. What went wrong in Venice Beach went right in Naples thanks to better city planning.

Back on land, two adobe homes are a reminder of the Spanish and Mexican colonial periods in Southern California. The one-story **Ranchos Los Alamitos** (1806), complete with blacksmith shop, has the distinction of being the oldest building in Long Beach. The Victorian interior design of **Ranchos Los Cerritos** (1844) comes as a surprise to the viewer, and echoes of both East Coast and English architecture can be found in the Queen Anne style **Bembridge House.**

A tour of the Palos Verdes and Long Beach area would not be complete without sailing to **Santa Catalina Island.** The place is a favorite with honeymooners, and it is easy to see why. Verdant as it was in Cabrillo's day, who discovered the so-called "Island of Saint Catherine" later named by Vizcaino, sunny Santa Catalina is a paradise for the ocean swimmer, sun bather, deep sea and underwater fisherman in addition to the rider and hunter. The picturesque hotels and stately casino of Avalon, the resort's only town, bring to mind an era gone by.

THE ORANGE COUNTY COAST AND PALM SPRINGS

South of Long Beach, the first stop on a coastal tour is the **Bolsa Chica Ecological Reserve,** a salt marsh nature sanctuary where one can catch a glimpse of many rare bird species. Then the Pacific Coast Highway leads to the surfing town of **Huntington Beach,** blessed by miles of sand and crashing waves. It was here, not Malibu, that surfing was introduced to the U.S. mainland from Hawaii, giving impetus to a craze that lingers still. National surfing championships are held here and there is even a **Museum of Surfing.** Fun on the beach often continues well into the evening, when barbecues are popular. The **Huntington Pier** is a favorite meeting place, as are the shops and restaurants of the **Pierside Pavilion** across Pacific Coast Highway.

The homes and shops in Huntington Beach are unpretentious, as opposed to the luxurious environs of **Newport Beach.** A quick glance at the beautiful Newport Harbor would lead one to believe that owning a yacht is a prerequisite for town residency. Sixty thousand people live year round in this world-famous recreational community, and between 20,000 and 100,000 visitors arrive each day during the summer months.

They come to see the new and vintage boats, including the wooden flat-bottomed dories used by fishermen in their early morning trips. Large and small craft alike participate in the **Christmas Boat Parade of Lights,** a spectacular event held after dusk for the entire week before the holiday.

Sheltered by Balboa Peninsula, Newport Bay contains several manmade islands, and the tiny **Balboa Island Ferry,** inaugurated in 1909, is used as a shuttle. Midway on the Balboa Peninsula is the much-photographed **Balboa Pavilion,** a elaborate Victorian-style beach house built at the turn of the century and restored in 1969. Once a fashionable location for bathing beauty contests, dances were held in the Pavilion during the big band era, and the annual **Balboa Hop** still commemorates this tradition. It is also a terminal for boats going to Santa Catalina Island. The Pavilion is also the setting for the annual **Flight of the Snowbirds** held every June in Newport Harbor, a race centered around 150 Snowbird class boats.

*As seen from the air, **Long Beach** is composition of **cityscape** and **seascape** in close proximity to L.A.*

Above, *the area around* **Palm Desert,** *carpeted by wildflower blossoms, belies its name in the springtime.* Top right, *a golf course in Palm Desert, a boom town rapidly rivaling Palm Springs as a successful resort. The best time to visit both places is from January through April, as the summer can be uncomfortably hot.* Bottom right, *tasteful wealth is the hallmark of* **Palm Springs.**

On the cultural side, the **Newport Harbor Art Museum** has a strong collection of abstract expressionist canvases, and occasionally hosts exhibitions of contemporary work. The Bauhaus-inspired **Lovell House** gave a boost to the career of Rudolph Schindler, its designer. Just south of Newport Beach is the **Sherman Foundation Center** in the lovely beach town of Corona del Mar. The Center has a library and a number of botanical gardens and conservatories: a Japanese tea garden, a section devoted to succulent desert plants, another to tropical flowers. and, of course, a rose garden.

The **Crystal Cove State Beach,** an attractive stretch of coast, is the prelude to **Laguna Beach.** Once a haven for artists and writers, Laguna Beach has definitely gone upscale, although its past heritage is carried forward by the downtown art galleries and bookshops. Art definitely comes to life in the summertime **Pageant of the Masters,** when famous art works of the past are depicted as living pictures. Town residents appear as silent and motionless participants on stage before painted backdrops, in a effective rendition of a famous canvas or sculpture

by masters of the Renaissance, Baroque and other movements.

Moving closer to San Diego, **Mission San Juan Capistrano** (1776) was the seventh religious outpost built during the Spanish colonial era under the supervision of Junipero Serra. A 16th century Spanish altar graces the **Serra Chapel,** although the mission is best known for the annual ritual of **swallows** returning home (sometimes yes, sometimes no) on March 19 from their winter refuge in South America.

To the east, **Palm Springs** is the undisputed queen of the Low (or Colorado) Desert. There is a swimming pool for every three residents, and two palm trees for every person, not to mention the numerous golf courses and tennis courts. After World War II movie stars and politicians contributed to the fame of Palm Springs as a resort and winter home (summer temperatures hover around 100° F). Others come to enjoy the benefits of the **mineral springs** discovered centuries ago by the Cahuilla tribe. Finally, don't miss the **Living Desert Reserve** in **Palm Desert** to see the native animals and plants.

Left, *watch out for the "jumping catci" at the* **Cholla Catcus Garden.** *The very spiny, tree-like catcus has a tendency to stick to whatever is in the immediate vicinity.* Above, *a* **Joshua Tree** *silhouetted against a desert sunset.*

JOSHUA TREE NATIONAL MONUMENT

The **Palm Springs Aerial Tramway** carries the visitor to the top of 8,516 ft. **Mount San Jacinto,** and to the reward of a panorama encompassing the **Joshua Tree National Monument,** which commemorates the Old Testament prophet. Joshua's exploits in the desert prompted a band of Mormons crossing the Mojave Desert here to name the 20 to 40 ft. yucca plant in his honor. The weary group even saw in the outstretched branches an allegory of the Biblical figure pointing heavenwards. Groves of Joshua trees are found in the Mojave (or High) Desert section of the monument, while the glorious blooms of spring **wildflowers** thrive in the Colorado (or Low) Desert. The **Hidden Valley** in the Mojave Desert is one place to find huge, colorful quartz boulders uplifted by volcanic activity, sculpted by the wind and time. The more desolate Colorado Desert is the habitat of **Cholla Cactus Garden,** a species famous for adhering to passersby. Visitor centers in Joshua Tree Monument are located near the town of **Twentynine Palms** and in **Cottonwood Springs,** two of four oases watered by underground springs.

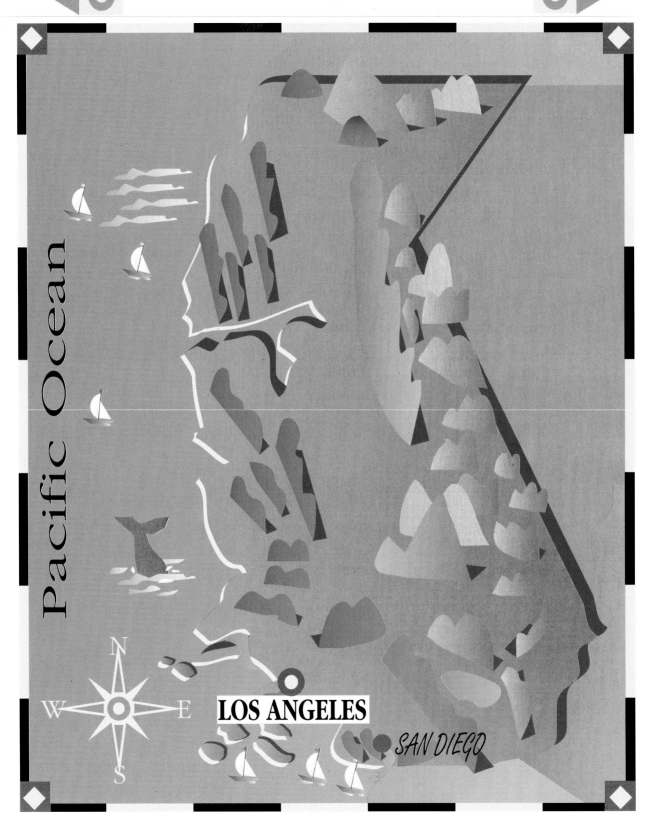

*A striking panorama of the **San Diego skyline** and **harbor** with the majestic mountains of the Cleveland National Forest in the background.*

SAN DIEGO

Simultaneously the first and last outpost in California because of its close proximity to Mexico, San Diego has enjoyed a boom in recent years. Near-perfect weather (the average year-round temperature is 70°) and a relaxed lifestyle have been among the major contributing factors. And, despite a population of nearly two and a half million, **San Diego** has maintained a distinctly small town charm. Rather than a compact, concentrated urban center, the city is a collection of smaller communities: Old Town, Coronado, Point Loma, Mission Beach and La Jolla are the most prominent. The city's excellent trolley system offers an alternative to cars and less convenient forms of public transport.

It's also hard to lose sight of the sea when in San Diego. Site of the 1992 America's Cup sailing competition, over 70 miles of Pacific coast make San Diego County an utopia for water sports and boating, and a network of freeways connects the beaches to downtown and other inland communities. Throw in nearby beaches, Sea World and the San Diego Zoo,

and you'll understand why tourism is now the city's third largest industry.

San Diego's excellent natural **harbor** turned the city into a bustling port town in the 1800s when Yankee trader ships began arriving to exchange manufactured goods for the cow hides and tallow of the Spanish-Mexican settlers. Today, yacht clubs, fish markets, restaurants and hotels crowd the waterfront. Seagulls fly overhead as seals swim among the boats. All types of seacraft fill the harbor waters, from houseboats and fishing boats to cruise ships and naval vessels. The downtown waterfront has seen particular development over the years thanks to the construction of the Embarcadero, Seaport Village and the Convention Center.

An inviting walkway beside the harbor, the **Embarcadero** stretches a mile or so from B Street and Broadway Piers south to the Embarcadero Marina Park in Seaport Village. Consisting of three fully restored ships docked at the Embarcadero, the **San Diego Maritime Museum** is another important harbor feature.

Without doubt, the most spectacular of the museum's exhibits is the **Star of India** (bottom photo,

Above, *the 1992 **America Cup races** were held in San Diego, and the city's Yacht Club was the defending champion. Top right, the **Hotel del Coronado** and guests playing volleyball on the stupendous Coronado Beach. The 19th century hotel was later expanded. No efforts nor artistic creativity were spared in its construction: the 33-ft. unsupported dome over the Crown Room is made of planks of sugar pine wood put together without nails. Right, the* **statue of explorer Juan Rodriguez Cabrillo** *on the tip of the* **Point Loma** *peninsula. There is a beautiful view of the San Diego Bay from here, along with the San Bernardino mountains in the distance.*

p. 156). A windjammer built on the Isle of Man and first launched in 1863, the "Star of India" made some 27 voyages around the world in its heyday. The iron merchant ship, retired from active service only in 1926, is now the oldest vessel of its kind still afloat. The other Maritime Museum ships are the **Berkeley,** an 1898 paddle wheel ferryboat, and the 1904 iron-hulled steam yacht **Medea.**

At the southern end of the Embarcadero is **Seaport Village.** A mélange of Spanish Colonial, Victorian and Old Monterey architectural styles, the beautifully landscaped village contains a variety of boutiques and restaurants. South of Seaport Village on Harbor Drive is the **San Diego Convention Center,** immediately distinguished from nearby buildings by its striking design.

Instead of a roof, the 100,000 square ft. top is covered with Teflon-covered white sails, and the overall effect is that of an enormous sailing ship rising up from the bay.

South of the waterfront downtown, across the San Diego Bay, is the island-like community of **Coronado.** Although characterized by the atmosphere and appearance of an island, virtually surrounded by waters of the bay and the Pacific Ocean, Coronado is actually at the northern end of a peninsula connected to the mainland. Coronado's most well-known monument is the **Hotel del Coronado,** a State Historic Landmark (top photo, page 151). The hotel's background is a fascinating one. Two wealthy businessmen financed the construction of the wooden edifice in 1888, which was completed in a speedy 11 months by hundreds of Chinese workers. Thomas Edison supervised the installation of the first electric system west of the Mississippi, and the gingerbread architecture of the period can best be described as an eclectic blend of New England, Spanish and Mexican elements. Celebrities, politicians, royalty and dignitaries have flocked to the "Del" (as it is called locally) to spend

Left, some of the innovative new architecture illuminating San Diego's expanding skyline at dusk. Above, the five-million-gallon capacity **Shamu Stadium** *is where Shamu, the three-ton killer whale, and his companions Baby Shamu, Namu and Nakina perform acrobatic feats for the public at* **Sea World.** *Right, one of the 30* **koalas** *at the San Diego Zoo in Balboa Park: more koalas than any other zoo in the U.S.*

their holidays ever since, and the hotel's evocative setting was even used as the location for the 1959 movie *Some Like It Hot,* starring Marilyn Monroe, Jack Lemmon and Tony Curtis.

West of Coronado are the rugged cliffs of **Point Loma,** a peninsula of exceptional natural beauty. On Point Loma's southern tip is the **Cabrillo National Monument,** established in 1913 in honor of the explorer Juan Rodriguez Cabrillo, who landed at Point Loma on September 28, 1542. The monument covers 144 acres of windswept pines and junipers. The original 1904 Cabrillo statue by Portuguese sculptor Alvario de Bree was replaced by a new one in 1989.

On the east side of Point Loma is the **Bayside Trail** for hikers, winding down the steep rock slopes past the old hunting grounds of the Digueno Indians. On the western coast are tidal pools which can be explored at low tide, home to flowering anemones, crustaceans, starfish and octopus.

*Located at the entrance to Balboa Park, the **Museum of Man** is one of the few original Spanish Colonial-style edifices left here from the 1915 Panama-California Exposition. Especially prominent is the 200-ft. **California Tower**.*

North of San Diego on the coast between Point Loma and La Jolla is the **Mission Bay Aquatic Park.** The area was an enormous tidal swamp until the 1960s, when it was dredged to form a man-made bay. Mission Bay has resort hotels, marinas, restaurants, amusement centers and marine life of **Sea World** (top photo, page 153). The aquatic shows are a major draw: killer whales, each weighing three tons, perform in Shamu Stadium, leaping as high as 24 ft. out of the water and thoroughly soaking the public in the front rows with their acrobatics. The moving sidewalk of the Penguin Encounter takes people past a glass-enclosed polar habitat housing Emperor Penguins from Antarctica. Visitors are allowed to feed the walruses, seals and sea lions, and the California Tidal Pool Exhibition is designed specially so that children can touch sea urchins, starfish and other shore life. Sea World aquariums also provide a habitat to sea

turtles, Alaska sea otters, piranhas, bat rays and moray eels.

More wildlife, this time of a land variety, can be observed at the world-famous **San Diego Zoo** in Balboa Park. Inaugurated in 1916, over the years the zoo has developed across hillsides and canyons, nine separate ecosystems closely resembling natural habitats. Animals can thus roam freely in areas enclosed only by moats, viewed by people from bus windows or on walkways. There is an African Kraal, a Latin American tropical rain forest, and in 1991 a bioclimatic exhibit called "Gorilla Tropics" was opened for lowland gorillas.

Other sights include the Flamingo Lagoon, the Reptile House, the Channel Islands Sea Lion Show, Bear Canyon, Tiger River, the enormous Scripps Aviary for rare African birds and the Hummingbird Aviary. But the zoo does not limit itself solely to animals. In 1991, its 128-acre tropical garden became an accredited botanical garden. The Skyfari Aerial Tram furnishes transportation 170 ft. over the treetops from one end of the zoo to the other. The more than 30 koalas (bottom photo, page 153) constitute the largest number of the Australian marsupial in a U.S. zoo.

Balboa Park itself was set aside by far-seeing city fathers in 1868. It was chosen as the venue of the 1915 Panama-California Exposition celebrating the completion of the Panama Canal. The Exposition Committee decided to refurbish the city's infrastructure and adorn Balboa Park with stately Spanish Colonial-style buildings (pictured on page 155). Decorated patios and fountains were added, as well as ornamental shrubs and trees. The Exposition was a success and the new architecture became a permanent addition to the park.

The **Museum of Man** is situated at Balboa's official entrance. With 67,000 items, the Museum of Man is considered to have one of the finest anthropological collections in the country. Towering over the museum is the blue and white tiled dome of the **California Tower** (page 154). Its magnificent 100-bell carillon chimes every quarter hour.

Between Mission Bay and Balboa Park is the **Presidio Park.** On July 16, 1769, Captain Gaspar de Portola and Franciscan father Junipero Serra founded here the first Spanish settlement in present-day California. Portola built a *presidio* (a military fortress), while Serra supervised construction of **San Diego de Alcala,** his first mission, relocated several miles inland to Mission Valley in 1774; all that remains is a church, bell tower and garden. Back to Presidio Park, there are only a few ruins from the Spanish Colonial era left, marked by mounds below the **Junipero Serra Museum.** This is founded on the site of the original mission. Museum exhibits include artifacts from excavations at the presidio, Spanish Renaissance furniture, manuscripts and diaries belonging to the protagonists of San Diego's early days. The **Serra Cross** commemorates the location of the first mission.

Below, *the* **Casa del Prado** *in Balboa Park.* Following pages: (top left) *sunset over the San Diego Harbor as seen from the southern end of the* **Embarcadero** *waterfront in Seaport Village,* (bottom left) *the Maritime Museum's iron windjammer* **"The Star of India"** *brilliantly lit at dusk in the San Diego Harbor;* (right) *the* **Junipero Serra Museum** *in Presidio Park.*

California

The Golden State

Eureka
(I have found it)

PACIFIC OCEAN

NEVADA

199 YREKA 97
Lava Beds National Monument
Goose Lake
CRESCENT CITY
Del Norte Coast Redwoods State Park
101
Mount Shasta
Weed
ALTURAS
Salmon-Trinity Alps Wild Area
Trinidad
Castle Crags State Park
Burney Falls State Park 299
Willow Creek
Clair Engle Lake
Shasta Lake
395
EUREKA
Ferndale
299
Shasta Dam
WEAVERVILLE
Wiskeytown Dam
REDDING
44
Lassen Volcanic National Park
Eagle Lake
44
Fortuna
Rio Dell
36
Humboldt Redwood State Park
36
36
SUSANVILLE
Garberville
RED BLUFF
Almanor Lake
395
5 99
QUINCY
Fort Bragg
ORLAND
Willits
Oroville Lake
OROVILLE 49
Donner State Hist. Monument
Reno
1
COLUSA NEVADA CITY
20
Truckee
UKIAH LAKEPORT
MARYSVILLE
80
Gold Country
Lake Tahoe
CARSON CITY
Cloverdale
20
Clear Lake
YUBA CITY
49
AUBURN
99
50
Middletown
5
PLACERVILLE
88
SANTA ROSA
Wine Country
SACRAMENTO
16
JACKSON
Calaveras Big Trees State Park
4
395
Bodie
Bodega Bay
80
NAPA
SAN ANDREAS
Yosemite National Park
Petaluma
Concord
99
49
Angels Camp
road closed in winter
Mono Lake
SAN RAFAEL
Muir Woods Nat'l. Mon.
RICHMOND
Columbia State Monument
SONORA
120
Sausalito
Berkeley
108 120
120
OAKLAND
STOCKTON
Yosemite Village
SAN FRANCISCO
Livermore
MODESTO
Mariposa Grove of Big Trees
6
Half Moon Bay
Stanford
Central Valley
MARIPOSA
99
Bishop
SAN JOSE
MERCED
101
41
SANTA CRUZ
Gilroy
Los Banos
Kings Canyon National Park
Watsonville
5
395
Sequoia National Park

5 U.S. Interstate
101 U.S. Federal
299 State
Capital
County Seat

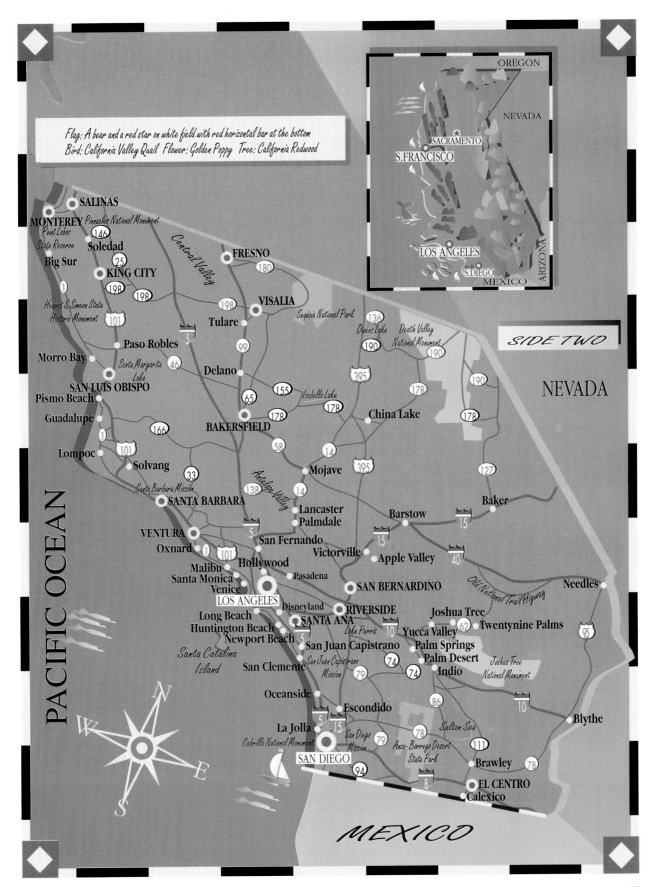

Flag: A bear and a red star on white field with red horizontal bar at the bottom
Bird: California Valley Quail Flower: Golden Poppy Tree: California Redwood

OREGON

NEVADA

SACRAMENTO

S.FRANCISCO

LOS ANGELES

S.DIEGO

MEXICO

ARIZONA

SALINAS

MONTEREY Pinnacles National Monument

Point Lobos
State Reserve Soledad

Big Sur 146

25

KING CITY

1

198 198

Hearst S. Simeon State
Historic Monument 101

Central Valley

FRESNO

180

198

VISALIA

Tulare

Sequoia National Park

136

Owens Lake Death Valley
National Monument

SIDE TWO

190

190

NEVADA

Paso Robles

Morro Bay

Santa Margarita
Lake 46

99

Delano

190

178

SAN LUIS OBISPO

Pismo Beach

Guadalupe

65 155

Isabella Lake

178

178

China Lake

178

Lompoc 101

166

BAKERSFIELD

58

14

395

127

Solvang

33

Santa Barbara Mission

SANTA BARBARA

Antelope Valley

138

14

Mojave

395

Baker

Lancaster
Palmdale

Barstow

15

VENTURA

Oxnard 1 101

5

San Fernando

Victorville

15

Apple Valley

40

Old National Trail Higway

Needles

Malibu
Santa Monica
Venice

Hollywood

Pasadena

SAN BERNARDINO

LOS ANGELES

Disneyland RIVERSIDE

Joshua Tree

62 Twentynine Palms

Long Beach
Huntington Beach
Newport Beach

SANTA ANA

Lake Perris 10

Yucca Valley

95

5

San Juan Capistrano

Palm Springs
Palm Desert

Santa Catalina
Island

San Clemente San Juan Capistrano
Mission

74

79

74 Indio

Joshua Tree
National Monument

Oceanside

Escondido

86

10

Blythe

La Jolla 5 15

Cabrillo National Monument

San Diego
Mission 79

78

Salton Sea

Anza-Borrego Desert
State Park

111

Brawley

78

SAN DIEGO 94

8

EL CENTRO
Calexico

PACIFIC OCEAN

N
W   E
S

MEXICO

159

INDEX